Farm Boy 101

A Memoir of Fifty Five Years Of Being A
Farm "Kid" In Southern Minnesota 1953-2008

DENNIS DOBIE

DEDICATION

This work is dedicated to my parents. Harold and Edna. Dad and Mom.
Pa and Ma. With great love from their youngest child son.

.

CONTENTS

ACKNOWLEDGMENTS

In writing this work, I have borrowed both liberally and literally from an earlier book I published. Plagiarism? Lawsuits? I'm not going to sue myself. Anyone who dislikes my perspective can write their own book. This is just a memoir from my own experiences.

Some people might get the idea that I'm trying to relive my "glory days." I don't know about that. For me, it's more than just reviving an old man's memories of past or lost youth. I'd prefer for the reader to view this as a tribute to the caretakers of the land they walked. From past generations towards future generations. The story lives on for every person in any walk of life. Each of us are only here for around eighty years of a fourteen million year old planet. It's how we live and what we leave behind that are the most important.

This story takes place in or very near to my parents farm in southern Minnesota, located about thirty miles north of the Iowa border and about 150 miles from either South Dakota and Wisconsin.

Southern Minnesota is in the heart of an agricultural country. Farmyards dot the landscape about every half mile or so, always with a grove of trees on the north and west sides to block the cold northwest winter winds. During the summers most of what you see in any direction are corn and soybean fields. During the winters, you see snow.

Quite a bit of this memoir story takes place during the summers. There are reasons for this. A great deal of farm work is done during the summer. That's also the time of year when a kid is not in school. More is expected from them then. And, let's face it, summer is just about the best season in a year. Much easier to remember than long days in a classroom, even though I loved school.

Summer in southern Minnesota. Blue skies that yielded to clouds and about an inch of rain each week. Twelve to fourteen hours of sunlight each day. Average temperatures near eighty degrees. A lake to swim or fish in at the end of our farm lane. We didn't know it then, but we had everything a person could ask for.

Everyone has a story to tell. I know of at least two other people who were writing outlines to explain "the story of my life." One of them had a good start by using their yearly holiday greeting letters. I'm not going to attempt my whole life story; it'd probably be too ambitious an endeavor and include a lot of things that others might not find all that interesting. Let's just say I bounced around a lot and stayed in adolescence for far too long. I'm also not going to delve into social commentary too much. There is always a great deal of political and apolitical drama occurring. Certainly, whether it's a time of peace or war; a time of liberal or conservative; a time of prosperity or struggle—there are influences on anyone's life. Let's not forget: we each are our own biggest hero AND villain.

I've always had difficulty with words like "I," "we," "they" etc. (This must be a first-person singular narrative indication.) The "I" in this true story happens to be my own personal memories and experiences. Who is the I? In this case it's just a Southern Minnesota farm and small-town kid who never really traveled much and was both naive, gullible, hardworking, possessing no great talent, and was fortunate enough to survive an interesting bunch of experiences. (To put matters into context, when I say small town, I mean it. I grew up on a family farm (200 acres, mom, dad, seven kids, and grandma in a house with one bathroom) eight miles from the nearest town, four of them to be exact. None of the towns had a population of over one thousand.

I went to school in Mapleton, MN. It doesn't really matter where a farm kid lives; this story could be told by thousands of others with different backgrounds than mine. Hopefully the tale will be interesting reading for some. I'll use the first names of real people for authenticity for the most part but not their last names for their privacy. My name is Dennis, or Denny, or as school students are supposed to call me, Mr. Dobie. (The last name is pronounced doe bee) In any instance, don't sue me, I have little to take except some interesting memories.

Please keep in mind that this document is a **personally biased memoir**. This is intended to be a memoir and only a memoir of what I was told, what I lived, and what I observed. This work is not a work of **researched history**. However, this stuff really happened.

And, of course, I don't really expect to make any money by writing this. It's just for my enjoyment, and possibly yours.

One more final thought. Before reading further you should not take any of the actions we did regarding raising of animals to the ASPCA. We weren't grooming pets. Our animals, for the most part, were headed to a slaughter house. They were to become food for somebody. If an animal got in our way we would just shove them off to the side. Certainly there were times when a slap, kick, or knock up the side of a head with a shovel was necessary. We took good care of our livestock, nothing overtly cruel. Somebody had to run the zoo and it wasn't going to be the animals. Sometimes it was just necessary to give them a push. Animals have different personalities just like people. Some of them just needed a little more persuading than others. It was expected.

Insert chapter one text here. Insert chapter one text here. Insert chapter one text here. Insert chapter one text here. Insert chapter one text here. Insert chapter one text here. Insert chapter one text here. Insert chapter one text here. Insert chapter one text here. Insert chapter one text here.

CHAPTER ONE
RAISED IN A BARN

It was sometime a few months after my twenty third birthday that a group of my peers gathered at a friend's house in my newly adopted hometown of Mankato, MN. I didn't realize that I was the last person to enter the home and didn't shut the exterior door after me. My friend whose house we had just entered told me to shut the door and asked if I was born in a barn. I told him "No, I was just raised in one." Being a city kid, my friend didn't catch my meaning so I had to explain it to him.

Yup, I was a Southern Minnesota farm kid trying out city life. Sometimes I wish I had stayed on the farm. I sure do miss it now. As of this writing I'm 68 years old and the farm is almost fifty years behind me. It's true what they say; hindsight is 20-20.

Our family farm was located only about thirty miles from the Iowa border. Looking at a map of Minnesota it was just about an equal distance from either Wisconsin or South Dakota. In terms of size I'll add a little background here. Land had been plotted out in square miles during the early nineteenth century. The idea was that there would be a road every mile and that ran pretty much true to form. One square mile was termed a "section." Each "section" was the equivalent of 640 acres. The early mostly European descent settlers either bought, stole, or claimed a quarter section of land which amounted to 160 acres. So, in every square mile there would be four family claims of land.

In the case of my family's farm, the "bought, stole, or claimed" statement is all true. The United States government had "bought" large tracts of land from Indigenous Americans who were mislabeled Indians. I'm not going to delve into too much politics here but the "bought" portion was basically also the "stolen" part. The United States government happened to be the one who had the biggest guns and forced indigenous Americans off of their land. That's not much different than any other land grab made by different nations throughout history; the civilization with the best weapons pretty much dictates policy when taking over a land area, leaving the former owners out of luck. I'm not saying this is right; it's just the way things have been.

Another part of "stolen" came when my great grandfather Joseph Dobie and his family arrived in the area. He did not have any prearranged plot of land promised to him as many settlers did around 1856. The Joseph Dobie family had traveled west to the Minnesota territory via a number of rafts and boats on various rivers. Once they got to the river town of Mankato, they obtained a short term family lodging and Joseph went on a twenty-five mile hike south. He found a parcel of land and used wooden stakes to notify others that it was his. The land had been legally promised to another settler but, like a lot of other people, Joseph and family got there first and took ownership.

There were a bunch of other people that got frustrated by land jumpers (like Joseph?) and just got back on the riverboats to try their luck in other places.

We'll get back to what I know about Joseph Dobie's background story a little later. Suffice to say that he got his 160 acres. It was not a square shaped acreage. It looked from the sky or plot maps to be kind of a lopsided L. On the eastern end of his plot was the shallow Lura Lake (Maybe 10 or 12 feet deep in the middle, maybe one hundred yards wide, and about a mile long) which cut in somewhat on his land. Somehow on the western end there was another 40 acre plot that came to be owned by another Dobie family member but I'm sure Joseph and family farmed it as well. I know my parents always did. My folks paid rent on that extra land, but we always walked it as if it was our own.

And the land was pretty much flat. There was one hill on the rented forty acres, but it was a gradual rise, just noticeable enough to put a little extra strain on the legs while the family members took hoes in hand in search of pesky weeds that would suck up the precious water from our soybean fields. The land did dip a bit further on the northwest corner where it started tapering off to one of our neighbors land which had a creek running through it. That's the area which tin cans and other refuse would be thrown into before the recycling era. The neighbors didn't seem to mind. They threw their old junk that wouldn't burn onto the same pile.

And the dirt was pretty much black. That is with the exception of that hill on the west side again where it turned a little more brown. This must have something to do with getting close to a water source, the land gets a bit sandy. I don't know if there is any truth to a story I heard about black soil, but there was a rumor that the ground was some of the best for growing crops in the world. It was explained to me when I was young that it was comparable to land in the country of Ukraine which had been the Sovlet Union's bread box for many years.

World renowned or not, it was good farmland. The black soil of my family's farm was located in the Minnesota county of Blue Earth. Going back a few hundred years, an early French explorer named LaSalle had found the ground near the Minnesota River close to what is now the city of Mankato. Somehow one of LaSalle's crew members thought it might be full of copper so they loaded a boat load of the earth and traveled back to France with their discovery. Evidently there was no copper in it so all they got was some good old black dirt and a page in the sixth grade Minnesota history books we were required to read.

I guess the town of LaSalle MN, population around 800, is his only other legacy.

And the land, in the time of Joseph Dobie and family, was pretty much all tall grassland and trees. It was guaranteed to be a great deal of work and risk to turn it into a self-sustaining farm but Joseph and his wife had a bunch of kids to help them out. Cleared trees were split into planks which, at first, were used to provide roof boards for a sod house. Extra trees became firewood. The sod was cut from the black earth and placed around the house and on the roof. Given there was probably no glass and definitely no plastic sheeting, whatever windows there were had to be covered by skinned animal parts. The more anterior the animal parts, the more light could come through. But, it was translucent light, not the transparent kind. In other words, although some light would come in, a person could not see out.

We can only imagine how tough those first years were. The barn I grew up in was still half a century away.

CHAPTER TWO
JOSEPH

As part of one of my somewhat distant Dobie cousin's masters degree courses, the gentleman did quite a bit of research into the family's past. The time frame on his research was probably in the early 1960's, long before a person could pay a fee, gather a drop of blood, search a dot com, and learn about their ancestry in a much easier and less costly way. Anyway, cousin Dobie and a few other local historian's noted some interesting details about Joseph and other Dobie's. If I could have found cousin Dobie's name and reference work I would have gladly included it here. He has my thanks instead.

Ronald J. Newell PHD deserves a great deal of credit for his book <u>Where the Winding Maple Flows</u>. A bit of information for this Joseph chapter filled in around the edges of what family stories I recollected.

Cousin Dobie knew, as all Dobie's did, that Joseph was born in Scotland. My mother recollected to me once that the name Dobie originally was a French name. The Dobie clan could have been from there. Mom indicated that French Dobie's moved to Scotland a few centuries ago to keep from being persecuted for their non-Catholic religion. The story might have had something to do with the Huguenot ideas about God. That's what a mom said, so this son dutifully believed her.

A trip to Scotland was taken by cousin Dobie. He found all sorts of graveyard headstones with the family name and dates on them. Another prevalent last name was Jardine. Given cousin's research, there seemed to be a number of Jardine - Dobie marriages. Maybe they were cousins also, who knows for sure?

During the 1700's in Scotland and other places, the oldest son got to keep the family's small farm land. The other kids had to make other arrangements. By the time my great grandfather Joseph was a fairly young man, (1840's or so) he had married and had some children. An opportunity arose. The term was indentured servitude.

There were a number of open positions for farm laborers in a relatively new country called The United States of America.   Probably through written correspondence, Joseph was hired to work on a farm in the state of New York. His employer paid the cost of the Joseph Dobie family's trans-Atlantic sailing boat voyage. In return, Joseph and family worked on the farm for little beyond food and housing for an extended number of years. Most of those contracts, if I remember correctly, were a seven year commitment. I believe Joseph got out of his in six.

Joseph was one of many people from Scotland who moved to Southern Minnesota in the mid 1850's. The town he was closest to was named Mapleton. It was located only a couple of miles from the Dobie farmstead and could somewhat easily be reached on foot or horseback during good weather, or by ice skating in the winter. Tie on a pair of blades, glide up the length of Lura Lake, walk a couple of hundred yards, then blade up again for the final skate up the Maple River to get to Mapleton's post office and small town store. There was only one unforeseen problem.

When the railroad company decided to run a line through the area, the small community of Mapleton was not on the path. What few people who lived in the village mostly got together, moved, and rebuilt the new Mapleton town to meet the new form of transportation.   Advanced technology, adaptation by the populace. Decades later, a school was built in Mapleton. In deference to the homeland of many of the original settlers, their sporting teams became known as the Mapleton Scots.

Joseph would probably have been a good sports athlete given any era. It has been reported that he was just under six and a half feet tall, wide shouldered, and strong. There were no football or basketball teams for Joseph. Heck, those games hadn't even been invented yet. Still, people adapt to their conditions as do their games. Scottish people enjoyed sliding heavy, smooth, granite rocks across the winter lake ice to score points, something like shuffleboard. So, the sport of curling came to be enjoyed by area residents of the time, and is still popular in Mapleton and other places in southern Minnesota.

I can remember a couple of these curling stones being stored in one corner of our farmhouse basement.   At around forty pounds each, they sure were heavy for a nine year old.

Minnesota became an official state in the USA in 1858. The American Civil War began a few years after that. In between these years there was a Native American Indian uprising in southern Minnesota that caused a great deal of strife and too much bloodletting for me to chronicle here. Like most of their neighbors, Joseph and family retreated to a different nearby town in case they were attacked. The fighting never made it as far south as the Dobie homestead but it was a great cause for concern. There was a definite threat. Who am I to judge? The Indigenous Americans had had their land stolen from them for a couple of centuries by that time. Land ownership and its loss can lead to some very hard feelings.

Somehow during those years, between mass production and a need for an armed citizenry, a muzzle loading rifle was given to each area farmer. The one that the Dobie family was given remains, to the best of my knowledge, in the family today. I can remember my brothers and an uncle firing it off a few times when I was just a kid. Joseph didn't have to fight in either of the aforementioned wars. By that time he had enough kids to take care of and his service was not mandated.

And Joseph's children grew up. When thinking of the late 1880's time period, a person should take into account that transportation was an issue. No one went too far or too fast. Socializing was done pretty close to home. It ended up that neighbors married neighbors. Joseph's children certainly followed this trend. As my parents grew up and even through my 1960's generation, we were shoestring related to a good percentage of the people in my hometown.

As noted elsewhere in this document, trees became timber which supported the roof of early farm buildings. Those would be walled and topped by sod which needed to be dug from the earth. The sod had, in my mind, to be around one foot cubes. Sod is basically dirt that is held together by grass roots and moisture. Try digging a one foot cube out of your lawn sometime using only a shovel. You'll come to a whole new respect for the amount of work that went into home building on prairie land.

Still, trees and sod weren't the only things that needed to be cut. The top two feet of Lura Lake ice was fair game as well. A great deal of chopping and cutting of it took place every winter. There was one building, half buried underground and with walls of sod to start with, that became a cold storage unit. Refrigerators hadn't been invented yet either. I could point out to a spot where the ice house had been at one time on the farm. I can't speak to its effectiveness. However, I can personally attest that on the eastern part of our land, where Lura Lake lapped up against a semi protected southern wedge of shoreline, I saw a snow and ice wedge into the month of June one year when I was a child.

Near any water source, a person will probably find trees. With a lake on the east side of our property and a creek near the west side, one could be assured that there was an abundance of them. At one time shortly before I was born there were so many trees near the lake that a lumber company set up a small saw mill on our property with my ancestors' blessing. I don't know how much of the wood processed became part of our home and out buildings, though I was informed that some of the deal for the lumber produced was part of it was given to the family. I wasn't around when the family machine shed was built but I had to fix up the huge quonset style building on a few occasions. I added new lumber to what was a definite native lake side product. Covered it with a bunch of tin a few times too.

The lumber company was happy. They had access to a lot of material to sell. Dobie's were happy. They received a lot of building material AND they had a great headstart on clearing more land for farming. It's nice when some things work out well.

Sod huts gave way to cabins. Cabins gave way to larger farm homes. Eventually, around 1900 or so, Joseph moved his family into a five bedroom home a little farther away from the lake. That's the building he died in. That's the building my father was born in. That's the building I was raised in; along with being raised in the barn which also came to be built at that turn of the century time.

At some point the red barn became adorned with large scroll white lettering proclaiming it "Queen of the Lake". Although the buildings were painted over several times and I never saw the scroll, I always was impressed with the idea of my beloved barn and farm being something special. Word eventually seeped down hill to me that it was more about a gimmick by a roving group of building painters. A barn at one of our neighbor's homes, about a mile from ours, had been painted and dubbed "Queen of the River."

Talk about shattered delusions of grandeur. There are times I wish I had not received some reality checks.

Still remaining of the Dobie and other settlers of Scottish heritage in the area is the name of the township. Right there in southern Blue Earth county, Minnesota, the township is known as Sterling. The official spelling of the township using an e in the middle was a land recorder's mistake. Many of the settlers had come from Stirling township in Scotland and wanted to honor their homeland. That's one typo that will never get corrected.

If a person is interested in the Stirling name, a thorough investigation might be in order. Either that, or watch a Mel Gibson movie or one about Robert the Bruce. Stirling was the name of one of the areas and castles being fought over, around, and through by the English and Scots in centuries gone by.

It just gave this old man one more thing to write about. But, that too was to be expected.

CHAPTER THREE
GRANDMA: ANNA

My grandmother was born in southern Minnesota around 1883. She had a twin sister that I don't know anything about. Her last name, I believe, was of Finnish origin. Somehow a story which made it into my brain was how, as a young child, a half a dozen Native American Indians would walk into her log home and take whatever food they wanted including half baked bread that was cooking in the wood fired oven. Considering it was just her, her sister, a mother and a father with a muzzle-loading rifle for protection, her dad would back his small family into a far corner of the one room house and offer no resistance. One shot could have led to a massacre. All things would be made right as a couple of days later the family would wake up in the morning and find a quarter of a recently butchered deer hanging from their porch ceiling. The family ate. The family survived.

Grandma Anna must have been in her early twenties when she married my grandfather whose name was I believe Horace Greely Dobie. Horace was the youngest child of Joseph and he had remained on the family farm. On January 9th, 1909 she gave birth to my father, Harold Joseph. Horace and Anna went on to have three more children, two girls and another boy over the next eight or ten years.

Oftentimes grandmothers are portrayed in the media and in real life as loving people that live in their own home. Their grandkids can't wait to go visit them and be spoiled a little more. That was not always the case as multi-generational families under one roof were more normal going back a hundred years or so. It was definitely not true about Grandma Anna. She stayed put in the family farmhouse until she was nearly eighty years old. Things change in eighty years.

I've often heard it said that it's not advisable to speak evil of the dead.

Still, there is always someone digging up dirt about past politicians. And then there are family politics as well. Grandma was not an easy person to get along with. She could be bossy, demeaning, and spiteful. I guess maybe that's where I got it from. My dad mentioned to me one time that she had pretty much driven Horace Greely to drinking large amounts of alcohol. Her husband either died or was buried on July 4th, 1926, 150 years to the day after the signing of the American Declaration of Independence. My father was seventeen years old. Dad had graduated from the local eighth grade country school a few years earlier. He had to take over running the farm, help raise three younger siblings, and deal with his mother. Grandma pretty much retired to her room and took her chamber pot with her. I imagine she helped out some but I know my dad had to do the majority of the work.

Of course this tough situation was to last for almost eleven years until my parents were married in April, 1937. Talk about interesting family dynamics, who was going to take the female lead part now? Dad and mom took over the one downstairs bedroom. Grandma had to move upstairs. Eventually dad's sisters got married and moved out of the house. His younger brother stayed and actually graduated with a twelve year high school degree. Mom and dad produced baby boys born in 1937, 1939, and 1940 to be followed by three daughters over the next nine years. Grandma stayed in the house.

And Grandma continued living in the house until the late 1960's. My parent's children always had one more adult telling them what to do. Grandma helped around the house a little bit. She excelled at sweeping underneath the kitchen table immediately after supper. Dad eventually took offense at having to move to accommodate her brooming habit while he might be in the middle of a conversation and Grandma went to her room. And Grandma stayed in the house. She probably went back to her crocheting and produced more doilies.

And, that's the way it was until the mid to late 1960's when she moved in with one of her daughters. That didn't last long. As I said, she was difficult to get along with, even with her daughter. Sometime in the early 1970's she eventually really retired into a nursing home about eighty miles from the farm place. I remember visiting her there once. She was actually nice to me, possibly because I was with a cousin who was her favorite grandchild.

At some point during the mid 1970's Grandma was involved in exacting one more do I dare say act of vindictiveness. Somehow she got the idea that dad had underpaid her when he purchased the family farm from her during the 1930's. It was very true that land prices had skyrocketed since those years, especially given the 1930's were depression era years. To put an end to the shenanigans, dad, his siblings, and Grandma signed an updated, legally binding agreement. Pa wrote out checks for, I suppose, about ten thousand dollars to each of the four of them. Peace at last? I'm not sure. I'd bet that dad still ended up with the majority of Grandma's nursing home bills.

Grandma Anna died in January of 1985 at the age of 101. She had outlived her husband by nearly sixty years. I joined my parents, siblings, cousins, and what few friends she had at her funeral ceremony. A couple of her great grandchildren played an off key musical tribute at the service. There was a short sermon followed by the internment. I don't remember where she was buried as the funeral service was about thirty miles away from the farm. Why did I attend the funeral? I guess it was for closure, for the family, for a good reputation, a moral obligation. A cynical person might say it was just to make sure that she was really dead. Perhaps Grandma Anna would have accepted this bitter logic.

Dad was a little put off about the final results. A few of his nephews and nieces received what was left of Grandma's possessions and money. Pa only ended up with the entire bill for the funeral and internment. He paid for that, just like he had always paid for most anything else that involved Grandma.

CHAPTER FOUR
DAD: HAROLD

As with any other person, my parents were the smartest people on the face of the planet. That is except for the early teenage years when parents are always considered to be the stupidest people around by their children— that's normal. In my case, my parents worked damned hard.

My dad didn't have much choice whether or not to work hard. Born in January 1909, about the same time Ford Motor Company began producing its first cars, Pa grew up in a time when horsepower quite literally meant using a horse for power. He probably didn't get a ride in a real automobile until he was near his teenage years.

Therefore, one can assume that Harold's early life wasn't all that much different than his father's. At a young age, I'm sure he was tending livestock and field crops. He would have quickly learned how to attach harnesses to horses and use them to pull whatever farm implements were needed at times through the fields or around the farm yard. Dad would have quite literally walked behind the horse(s) with about a sixteen inch, one blade plow he had to push down upon to turn the field soil over. Quite a work out. Quite a muscle builder. It was expected.

As a child, I found one farm implement dating back to my dad's horse drawn days back in a corner of a shed. One of my older brothers told me it was an old cultivator. There was a metal bar that would have been attached to a horse's harness that extended back to another perpendicular, horizontal bar. The second had short arms extending from it every thirty six inches which each ended with a V shaped metal plate. The entire width of the implement was about six feet across.

Evidently seed corn was planted at three foot intervals in rows three feet wide. This horse drawn cultivator would dig out weeds which sprung up between the rows of corn. And, it could be used in all four directions in a field. Cultivate north to south and back. Cultivate east to west and back. A lot of walking once again. Do whatever it takes to get rid of weeds and increase the corn yield.

To put this into perspective, by the 1960's corn seeds were planted in rows thirty to thirty six inches wide with seeds placed about every foot. Quite an increase in seed and yield.

There will be more about Harold's early year farm work life in other areas of this book. Let's skip to the more social side. There wasn't much of it as compared to future generations. It was a matter of mobility. By the time dad was born, public education was mandated. So, like all of the other neighbor kids, Dad would have walked the mile or so to the local one room schoolhouse for grades one through eight. There he would have learned the "three R's", reading, riting, and rithmetic. Pa would have received some kind of certificate of attendance, a diploma or such after grade eight. That was it. Attending high school was out of the question as the closest one was eight miles away.

At some time in his preteen years while doing an outside farm task, dad took a blow to his side and had a heck of a pain. He somehow made it back up to the house and collapsed on an old couch that sat on the open front porch. Harold laid there for three days while his parents begrudgingly fed him, even though he couldn't work; they were probably miffed about that. After the third day, his parents finally took him to see a doctor who diagnosed a severely bruised kidney. Maybe there was medicine. Maybe there were ice packs. Maybe it just took time to heal. Probably his inability to help out on the farm for a week didn't help with either family dynamics or family economics.

And, his labor would have been needed on the family farm. He had to help his father and mother, and assist with the raising of his three younger siblings. As noted elsewhere, this was essential given the early death of Harold's father when Harold was only seventeen years old.

My dad never talked much about his youth, especially socializing. His parents evidently never went to church and Pa was never baptized. (Maybe that was a reason why I never heard him say the word "God" without an expletive attached to the end of it.) Too bad, churches would have been a major contributor to getting to know other people. Still, Pa got around some. He played catcher on the township baseball team. One of the few times he chatted about things like that to me he told me it was always tough to milk cows the day after a ball game. Too much squatting.

One story Pa did relate to me happened when he was still a growing boy. It seems that a traveling circus was making the rounds of small towns in the area. His parents probably didn't have either the money, interest, or inclination in attending such an event so they never went to a performance.

However, this was before trucks and paved highways were commonplace for transporting any items, including circus beasts. It seems that the horses and elephants pulled wheeled wagons full of personal housing, lions, tigers, and bears, etc from one town to another. This was bound to be a slow process as the line of carriages several city blocks long wound its way from town to town.

Such a lengthy progression would have interrupted what traffic there was on main roads. I also imagine that the circus owners would have looked on Minnesota road maps for the shortest back road distance, about twenty five miles, between Winnebago and Mapleton. That just happened to include the gravel road past the Dobie homestead. Dad stopped work long enough to watch the impromptu parade passing by. It's possible the entire family viewed the event. Perhaps grandma Anna approved, but I question that.

There were occasional dances in town on Saturday nights that he attended. He learned to flirt with the neighborhood girls like most other guys. One lady he dated just happened to have a younger sister that caught pa's eye. Guess which one he married. It didn't matter that mom was seven years younger than dad. That was a fairly common occurrence during the 1800's and 1900's. Women mature much more quickly than men. I suppose most men actually needed the extra years then to strike out on their own and have a place in the world before feeling successful enough to seek and support a mate and family.

A piece of legislation was passed by congress and the states while dad was a preteenager. He grew up in the times in which the production and consumption of alcohol was prohibited. I can guarantee that there were ways around this. Especially on farms that were eight miles from town. Fermenting has been around for a long time. Most people have had a sip or two at some point in their lives. I don't think that was ever an issue with pa. Maybe it was because he had seen what it had done to his father.

I've seen some pretty tough economic cycles during my years on this planet, but they pale in comparison to those which my father's generation endured. Dad would have been twenty years old in 1929 when the stock market crashed and the great depression took around a ten year grip on the entire world. There was no margin of error for anyone. In retrospect, it was lucky that Pa lived on a farm. At least his family could eat.

It was related to me by a different depression era survivor that they ate potatoes. Evidently, when nothing else would grow, potatoes would and became a staple of their diet. This was most important during the drought dust bowl years of the 1930's. Little rain, lots of blowing dirt.

Fate provided one partial solution for struggling crops farmers like dad. There was Lura Lake at the east end of his farm. The lake did not have a river or stream running into or out of it. It was spring fed, the lake basically sitting on top of raised ground where no lake should have existed. During the 1930's, the lake just about completely dried up. There was still a little bit of moisture in the extended shoreline. So, that's where pa's corn field fared the best. He planted crops into what should have been and now is again a lake bed.

This was not a time of profit. This was a time of survival. In the cities, people lined up for a free bowl of soup at a Salvation Army type organization. People would stand on street corners with placards hanging from their shoulders proclaiming themselves willing to work just for food. At some point during these times one of our farm neighbors was relying on their sons to take care of their land. When the two sons were conscripted into military service, the neighbor lady hired dad to milk her cows for her. Pa received one dollar a week for his services. As times got tougher, she could only afford fifty cents a week. Dad still had to milk her cows. It wasn't much of an income, but it was steady.

In 1937, Pa got around to marrying Ma. They quickly produced sons in 1937, 1939, and 1940 followed up by three daughters in the 1940's. As noted elsewhere, I showed up in 1953. By that time dad was forty-four years old. He grumbled to me one time later that with that many mouths to feed there was a year or two where the family had to butcher nine hogs and one beef just to feed them. The kids all learned to work but I know none of us worked as hard as dad. I'll write about bits and pieces of his abilities in other places in this book.

It still amazes me how strong he was. At five foot and maybe nine inches, and maybe 170 pounds, he could use his muscles all day every day. And he was still limber and flexible. After bending over working with soil and livestock, especially milking the cows for so long, he could still at the age of sixty bend straight down at his waist and place his hands flat on the floor. It makes my back hurt just thinking about it.

Yes, Pa worked hard. He had what I call the "one more round" theory. Now, one more round could mean a lot of different things to a lot of different people. It could be more playing time for a golfer. It could mean last call for a drunk. For my dad it meant by driving the tractor and plow once more around the field in the evening, he would have less work to do the next day. And that's the way it was while I was growing up in the 1950's, 1960's, and 1970's.

To be sure, Dad figured that his kids could put in an extra round as well. One of the jobs I liked least was walking the soybean fields. They could be run through with a tractor pulled cultivator to remove weeds during their first month of life. After that, in June and July, it was sheer human and hoe time. Pa would enlist Ma and whatever kids were at home at the time and we would spread ourselves out four rows apart and start walking. Back and forth a quarter mile field we would trapse digging and hacking out weeds.

Most of the weeds we could uproot with our hoes. Sometimes they were just a clump of corn that had been missed during the previous fall harvest. It's interesting to note how many different kinds of weeds we would find. And, they all had different names. One unusual plant we called a "mustard" weed. They were somewhat yellow and had hollow roots. The perfect things to make kazoos out of. That was about as much fun as we could find out there.

For the most part, we could just chop out the offending plants with the exception of cockelburr and button weeds. Because of their ability to grow, mature, drop seeds quickly, and their large broad leaf size, these two types had to be dug out and carried to the end of the field closest to the house. After drying out for a few days, the pile would be burned.

My parents knew the names of most of the weeds we would cut out of the fields. When in doubt, they would call the thin ones "some kind of water weed". One broadleaf weed was called milkweed because of the white gooey substance that was found inside its stalks. The "milk" they produced was actually a good remedy for covering scratches and scrapes or possibly just as a suntan oil. We would spread it liberally on our skin at times. Little did we know at the time that milkweed was the staple food for beautiful monarch butterflies. In the early 21st century, both were in decline, possibly on the endangered species list.

So, while the town kids were either running and playing or earning just a bit here and there doing odd jobs, I walked bean fields with the family. I never did get very good at running. But, the members of my family could walk and work at a steady pace all day long. And we would walk the bean fields for about a week. A couple of weeks later, we would walk them again.

Luckily (?) we never started walking beans until around nine AM. That was after morning chores were done and we had all eaten breakfast. A noon time break was always taken for lunch. And, we always left the field by four PM. Then it was back to the barn for afternoon chores.

The corn fields didn't need much walking to get rid of weeds. By the fourth of July the corn plants would sometimes be close to shoulder high, especially for a ten or twelve year old kid. We just didn't have to go through them. Besides that, the corn would grow taller than the weeds, unlike soybeans. Corn plants reached up to ten feet high by the time they were harvested. Soybeans might make it to four feet.

I'm not sure if Pa ever planted any sweet corn crops although they were in demand by the local crop canning company in Winnebago. One year Dad did plant a thirty plus acre plot with peas in coordination with the canning plant. In mid summer, the company sent out specialized pea harvesters and a bunch of trucks into the field. A canning official stood right next to Pa and counted the number of truck loads taken from the field. Somehow the official's tally was one less than Dad's total. That one truck would have provided a profit. Thirty plus acres produced a break even income. What a waste. We grumbled about that one for a week while we did the evening chores.

There are a couple of other things I need to add in here. As far as I can remember, Dad always did the morning cow milking, livestock feeding, and egg gathering chores by himself. Maybe his kids had to help with some early day work, but for the most part, he never pushed us too much for assistance. It's interesting now, in the 21st century, child and school experts suggest that teenagers start school a bit later in the morning than grade school age kids. Something about a physical or psychological phase or such. Maybe Dad knew something intuitively that child experts came to know. Maybe Dad just enjoyed doing the milking without annoying kids in the way.

One fine summer morning in 1970 it was going to be a bean walking day. It was going to be a hot, humid bean walking day. My parents had quite a time trying to find me; I was hiding out in the cool basement. By that time I was sixteen years old and had my own car. Given my inherited vindictiveness, when found I swore to my parents that if I was herded out into the bean field they had better not turn their backs on me or I'd be driving away down the road. After having vented my displeasure, we all ended up chopping out weeds all day. Nothing ever came of it.

One thing is for sure from walking beans and other field work. I learned to know every square inch of that farm land.

And if we were not walking beans or baling hay or doing some other farmwork, what then? With a little luck the kid portion of our family would walk bean fields for neighbors and actually get paid a bit. A dollar or two a day in the 1960's meant a great deal to a farm kid then.

Groups of kids bean walking in the late 20th and early 21st centuries has become a thing of the past. There have been many advances in seed plant genetics which make them more resistant to weeds. And, who needs to hire walkers when a single farmer can mount a small spray tank and hose onto a small all terrain vehicle and just shoot out a weed killer chemical spray? The farmer can also deduct the expense of a fun driving machine from their income taxes.

There are many chemicals in use on farms. Besides weed killers, many chemicals are yield raisers. The more bushels of crop produced, the higher amount of money earned. Either easy, the chemicals don't stay in the ground forever. Rain and streams run them downhill. Pollution? Don't say the word.

It's with great pride that I remember coming home to the farm from college in 1973 one Friday evening. It was just after six PM and my father, who was by that time in his mid-sixties, drove his tractor and plow into the farmyard. He got out to have supper. He intended to go back out and finish the thirty-acre patch we had just to the north of our farm site but he looked at mom and wearily said "I just can't do it." How does a twenty year-old college kid respond to something like that? I drove that diesel until after three in the morning to get the field plowed before the snow that was predicted for the next day. A college kid at three in the morning? It wasn't all that much later than I was used to staying up anyway.

Yes, I became a college kid, but earlier in this work I mentioned both Ma and Pa attending a one room country schoolhouse. It is interesting to note that what goes around, comes around. Five of my six older siblings also attended the same country school. Dad even told me about his time on the local country township school board. At the end of one year, while going through the accounting books, the board members found a discrepancy of one penny. It took at least three meeting reviews, and they still couldn't find the mistake. I imagine someone finally got frustrated enough to donate the extra copper coin just to finally balance the books..

It seems that one room country schools had difficulty keeping teachers. They didn't pay well. At one point, the teacher would be shuffled from one farm home to another monthly if not weekly as part of the "room and board" provision of the contract. (Not in our district) Parents and their kids often didn't give the teachers enough respect; that will probably never change. But the biggest problem was that the teachers were often young ladies, just out of a two year teaching program from a local college. It didn't take long before the new teacher would become some young single farmer's new bride. School marms just didn't last long on the job. I know, I grew up next to a couple of these ladies and their very happy husbands.

Pa also spent quite a few years as one of the township board members. Once in a while people would stop by for advice or a question regarding a road. One of them got a little heated, right on our front door step. Dad returned to the house, frustrated, but he didn't give an inch. The other guy left our property.

For some inexplicable reason, even into the 1970's, the township was required to have a "Justice of the Peace." It was more of a ceremonial position than anything, nobody ever was expected to take up a gun and probe crime scenes. One year, one of the kids I had raced bicycles with as a youth, was just old enough to be elected to the position. Near the end of his term, right before the state law changed, a young couple stopped by his house wanting to get married. My friend was bound by legal authority. The couple had a wedding license. After a couple of "I do's", he told them, "OK, you're married." Maybe they still are.

There's an old saying that "You can take the boy out of the country, but you can't take the country out of the boy." I'm talking about 20th century family farms where a quarter section, 160 acres of land, would be enough for a family to subsist on. In many ways, it WAS a business but on a smaller scale. Kids worked the farms with their parents. Livestock and machinery were big investments. All too often, profits were minimal and needed augmenting by taking on extra jobs.

One thing is for sure, growing up that way made people in those families self-reliant. We had to fix machinery, care for animals, and walk the land with a hoe handy to cut out nasty weeds that would suck the water from the crops we needed to grow. If there was a job to do, most of the time we just had to do it. It was expected.

Given self reliance and a good work effort, I found my way through many different job scenarios during my post farm life. Whether I grumbled my way through this chapter or not, I owe a lot of personal life success to my dad.

Pa would occasionally grumble too. He was frustrated by his lack of education that only allowed him to be a "dig in the dirt" farmer. (At one point he advised me to become a school custodian because they earned decent pay and didn't have to work so hard. I passed up this idea, although I was offered a school janitor job at one point, and went on to be a school teacher instead. The teacher's salary was better, the work was great although stressful.) In the mid 1970's I had to explain to Dad that he and Ma together were worth a million dollars.. All of those acres, livestock, and all of those machines. All of the work. In straight out monetary value, he got farther than I ever did. Dad scoffed at the idea. But, it was true.

And Dad's sons? Three of the four of them, including me, approached Pa with the idea of going into business with him. We wanted to be involved in the farming process. We were all told "no" to the idea of expanding the family business. Maybe it was because he had seen too many other family farms that had had financial difficulty with expansion. Perhaps it was because he had lived through such traumatic times as the depression and didn't want to go through tough times again. It probably was because he wanted us to make more of ourselves than farmers. In any case, only one of his sons went on to start his own farm and eventually rented Pa's acres when Dad semi-retired. Maybe that was expected.

Still, dad had farmed his own land into his seventies. How many other people work that long? He'd be out there driving his tractors and trying to move augers and elevators into place. The rent money he received for his crop land went a long way as cash for his retirement. I'm glad he had this reward after working with such effort for so long. His often times grouchy mood and non-cussing vocabulary improved without so much stress. Golden years. Good years.

There are thousands of other words I could write here. They wouldn't be enough.

Dad.

CHAPTER FIVE
MOM: EDNA

Edna Ella was born on August 20, 1916. Her last name was either Stuemke or Steumke, either way I probably just misspelled it. She was destined to marry my dad and raise seven kids, she just didn't know it.

Mom was raised in both northern Illinois and southern Minnesota with two brothers and two sisters. Evidently her father and mother moved their family back and forth between the two state areas a few times. I can envision the opening scene of a hillbilly show, driving around on country roads in a dilapidated truck. More probably trains provided transportation. It was difficult to leave their Illinois cousins. Eventually, her parents put down roots on a farm not far from where I was raised. Both of my mother's parents were of second generation German extraction. And, they spoke German in their household.

Mom didn't learn to speak English until she went to the mandated public school education system.

My grandfather Stuemeke, another misspelling, was a combination farmer, carpenter, and musician. I believe he enjoyed carpentry work the best but couldn't really make a living at it. He became a farmer, like so many others at that time, just as a way of making sure his family got fed. And the musician grandfather, well he had talent with stringed instruments, produced a family band, and performed at local functions during his lifetime.

I ended up with some of his musical ability and band membership. The band part is another book.

So, my mom was a farmgirl and did farmgirl things like helping with chores, working with animals (I know she could put a harness on a horse), and probably flirting with farmboys. She was plenty smart as well. After graduating from the one room schoolhouse eighth grade, she was encouraged to attend high school. This was going to take quite a bit of doing as she was at least eight miles from the nearest town that had a ninth through twelfth grade school. Transportation was going to be the determining factor.

Edna found her way around this situation. At age fourteen, she traded her services of being a nanny to a family who lived in town for room and board at their house from which she could walk to school. So, she became the more highly educated of my parents. She made this work through ninth grade. By this time she would have been a slim five-foot-seven. Her folks probably appreciated her help around their farm.

Evidently the young grade school age boy she was supposed to care for was quite a handful. The term spoiled brat seems to apply. After one year of this experience, mom never went back. There were more than a few times when, as a child, I would have a nasty attitude, and Ma would relate her story of nanny times to me. Would I get a swat on the tush? What do you think? Did I deserve one? Again, your judgment.

Dad had actually been dating mom's older sister off and on over the years. A flirt? I don't know, probably some. You and I didn't invent love stories, just check out Romeo and Juliet. In any event, in January 1937, Pa walked a mile across our field, across a frozen creek, and across his neighbor's field with an engagement ring. Ma said yes. There was a short engagement period and a quick marriage ceremony. By the end of 1937, there was a baby boy. By the end of 1940, there were three baby boys.

One can only imagine the life adjustment my parents went through. Mom would have moved into a home that housed my grandmother (you already know my opinion) and three of dad's younger siblings. At one point Ma had had enough of the household political situation, grabbed whatever boys she had, and moved to a rented home about fifteen miles away. Pa soon followed. After a short period of time and some kind of reconciliation process, they ended up back on the farm again. Maybe Grandma realized she couldn't run it by herself.

And then there were the boys again.

Around the house was what we called the backyard. This would have been about a half-acre sized area between the home and the gravel road that ran alongside it covered in grass and trees. It was enclosed by white woven wire fencing that stood about three feet high. That helped to keep the animals out. It also helped keep the kids in. During the summertime, Ma would scoot her three young boys out the door and let them run around and play naked. That's something you'd probably get arrested for now, but, in the 1940's, it just made sense. It would sure save money on clothing. It saved on outhouse trips too. Little farm boys are experts at peeing behind a tree.

Before the reader gets all riled up about immorality, I will immediately add this. Mom made sure the kids had clean clothing on when she took them to church. Pa wouldn't go along, so Ma had to drive them. She found one Lutheran church in a town eight miles away that had a helpful congregation and attended it every Sunday until she could drive no more. Ma was active in the church, taught Sunday School, and could always be counted on for help with congregational dinners and other events. And, her kids all completed the confirmation process.

Later in life, Ma enjoyed it when I'd bring my children out to see the folks and occasionally have a meal. Mom would scoop up whichever kid was the youngest and sit the kid on her lap to share lunch with. Edna had had a lot of practice at this after having seven children of her own in a sixteen year time span. She was used to having a lap baby or child during meals.

One of my first memories of a trip to town in the mid to late 1950's was either going to church or the grocery store. We had a black car. Virtually every other car on the street was black. I remember talking to my sisters and telling them that our car was the prettiest black car on the block. Then, we'd actually see an automobile or two that was a different color. This would change a mind about a relative term like "prettiest."

Yes, Dad was kind of a stay at home person. He kinda had to. Pa'd either have a chore to do or would be too tuckered out to go anywhere in the evening. Mom made sure the kids were involved in social situations. She was the one who drove and supervised her children at 4H monthly activities. Occasionally, she would push Pa into going with her for town 4th of July fireworks displays or other small city celebrations. There was even one time when she loaded up all of the kids and took them to see a movie in town. The only reason I bring this up is because the only time I ever saw snow during the month of September was when I was preschool age. Snow knocked down power lines. We were bored sitting around a kerosene lantern in the farm's chilly kitchen. A Three Stooges film seemed like a good idea.

By the 1950's, the household had changed. Dad's sisters married and moved out. His younger brother had survived World War Two and hung around the house possibly to decompress for a while, eventually buying some land right next to our farm. Uncle had been trained in using artillery by the US Army, but didn't trust his commander whose last name was Patton. So, Unc volunteered with the Army Air Corp and ran one of the machine guns in a bomber, making ten around fifteen successful trips over France and Germany.

During the early part of World War Two, bomber crews that survived twenty five missions would not be required to continue to go on any more raids. That changed a little later in the war, more missions were expected as bombing intensified and there were only so many crews that could be trained and equipped at any given time. The attrition rate must have been horrible. A goal of twenty five missions was unlikely to be realized. Uncle's plane was shot down. He and six of the other ten men on it made a single parachute jump and all were captured by the German army immediately. Six months or more in a prisoner of war camp. Uncle went from 135 pounds down to 97 by the time his camp was liberated.

Uncle, as did the other POW's, needed some serious medical and nutritional attention before being healthy enough to be shipped back from Europe to the United States. Unc refused to ride in an airplane for the rest of his life.

Yeah. Uncle needed to decompress on the farm.

Pa and Grandma spent several months of 1944 and 1945 not sure if Uncle was alive. One of the other bomber crews could only attest to seeing seven parachutes come out of his plane. The Army didn't have much information; they had hundreds of thousands of people to keep track of. It took months before a brief letter from Uncle exchanged hands between Germany and Minnesota before my folks even knew if he had survived.

I'd guess my folks needed to decompress a little also.

Grandma still lived with us, but let's not go there. Dad and mom had a houseful of kids. The kids wore, for the most part, homemade clothing with the exception of jackets and blue jeans. Running this part of the operation was Edna. Don't get the wrong idea about the jackets and blue jeans being new garments. They were hand-me-down clothes from one kid who outgrew them to the next kid they would fit. Anything that just plain wore out would be cut into smaller pieces and used to patch the next pair of jeans or jacket. Ma patched the clothes. Sock holes would be restitched.

Toys would be shared between kids and handed down too. Youngest son was considered spoiled because he got new toys to play with. No surprise there, all of the older kids toys had been worn out by then. One exception was an old electric train set, circa 1945, which survived and was enjoyed by the youngest kid also. It was fun to take apart and put back together, keep it running. That lasted until the youngest son was about twelve. An older, well-meaning brother turned a four by eight sheet of plywood into a nicely painted landscape that was placed over the top of the pool table. Older brother permanently screwed down the train track onto the plywood. No more taking apart and putting together. Not much fun anymore.

Meanwhile, Harold was outside much of the time tending to the farm. When one or the other of them needed help, they relied on each other as well as the kids.

Sometime around 1960, dad got his tractor stuck in a field east of the house while plowing. Uncle lived next door. He tried to pull Pa's tractor out. He got his tractor stuck too. By that time, the older sons were gone and the youngest son didn't know about tractors. Mom knew about tractors. She helped find an area of dry ground. Pa hooked up the chains. It was quite the show. Ma rescued both Uncle and Pa.

Mother also had her own field. Okay, it was just the family garden, but it was quite a garden. Measuring in around thirty feet by seventy feet, it took up a chunk of the acre sized backyard her sons played in. There, she supervised the growing of just about every vegetable that a farm family could eat. With the exception of sweet corn. We didn't bother with that. We'd just go grab some ear corn from the crop fields when it had matured the right amount. Tasted the same to me.

So, the garden provided fresh summertime produce for the family. This was especially true when it came to salads. If we wanted a lettuce salad, no problem, just go pluck enough leaves from the garden. Going back to the hay bales days, summer family lunches usually included radishes and small onions.   Adults and kids alike got a few of each along with their personal salt dish. We'd dip the veggies into the salt and munch away. This has something to do with replenishing the salt our bodies would sweat away on warm days.

One of mom's specialties was what my dad nicknamed "bellyache". Somehow she could combine cucumbers, onions, and vinegar in perfect amounts and produce a salad that was unbelievably delicious. We probably all had breath that smelled like old iguanas, but no one could pass up on that dish.

Of course a lot of the peas, beans, potatoes, and more would end up being canned for winter consumption. This would be quite a process for Ma and her daughters and involved a great deal of cooking, steaming, jarring, and melting wax to seal up the mason jar lids. I stayed out of the way for most of that. I probably was a runner, a person who carried the produce from the garden to the house. Then, I'd hide. Typical kid. Trying to skip out of a job. That's the kind of behavior that crosses all cultures in all centuries.

Another side note: This was during the 1950's and 1960's. House jobs were pretty much covered by the females in families. Outdoor jobs were the work for the males. There was crossover when assistance was needed, but otherwise the women - men work was mostly defined by gender as it had been for more centuries than I could ever know about. I'm glad that this has changed since then, just for the expanded opportunities of both genders.

Sometimes whole meals could be canned. Mom had a way of cooking stew meat and using it and its gravy with potato and carrot wedges. Somehow this would also end up in a mason jar and be placed in one of the basement rooms. In the middle of the winter we'd have access to instant beef stew. And the wonderment of the canning process was that not only did it never spoil, it was never refrigerated either. The more a society advances, the more it should look into the past. My parents knew more about natural chemistry than I've ever learned from other teachers.

So, we've covered the veggie canning. There were also fruits grown in the garden area which needed to be preserved in the canning process. The garden was bordered on one side by a line of raspberry bushes which grew up and intertwined with a woven wire fence. Another section contained a good number of strawberry plants. And, off the end of the garden, stood at least two or three different apple trees. Back to the kitchen, back to the canning.

Then, just when a person would think they had stocked up well enough, crates of fresh peaches and pears would be delivered to the local grocery stores near the end of the summer. Of course, our family would purchase at least a crate of each. Once again, I'd hide.

Dad advised me about gardens a couple of times. They took up quite a bit of time and effort for the gains garnered. He'd tell me, as an adult, not to plant one. I'd explain that I had children who could help. He put gardening this way "when the kids are small you can't keep them out of it, when the kids grow up, you can't get them into it." Experienced parental wisdom is tough to beat. After a few attempts on my own I'd have to agree. But by the time I was a young adult we could get our pick of any canned goods we wanted from the grocery store. As a child on the farm that was not always the case. It was just another example of how independent and self reliant we were. We grew most of our own food.

Even given that, I had it easy. At one time our maple trees would have been tapped into for their syrup to satisfy the family sweet tooths. Flour would have been ground up from the farm's wheat crop. Spices may have been limited to those which grew in the garden.

That was not the case as I grew up. The family would purchase flour, sugar, and spices at the grocery store. Even as a child, mom would still bake our own bread occasionally. Mostly we relied on the bakery in town.

Pa always had to have bread and butter on the table for every meal.

I know dad got in on some of the garden process. It was a team effort. He would have helped with the planting, weed hoeing, and picking of the produce. Every fall he'd plow up the garden area being careful not to delve into the perennial raspberry, strawberry, and asparagus patches.

There were plenty of other times that my parents had to cover their spouse's duties. While reading this, you'll have to remember that dad had lived for forty four years and mom was thirty seven by the time I was born. I was an uncle at age seven. It was kind of like growing up with grandparents. As people age, their bodies sometimes need fixing. Every few years one or the other of them would end up ill which sometimes meant a short hospital stay.

It might have been on one of these occasions, or it might just have been mom was too busy to get to town and dad had to do the grocery shopping. What's the most important kind of paper in the world? Of course the answer is toilet paper. Another good reason to recycle publications, notebooks, and envelopes? Maybe. Back to the story. Pa found a bargain on one shopping trip. He chose to purchase, honest to God, the "Why Pay More" brand of toilet paper. It did a good job, with the consistency near some of the outhouse corn cobs that were used in dad's youth.

Mother was not pleased. After that, she always bought two packages of the soft stuff to keep on hand in case she had to miss a week in the future.

By default, Edna had to become a hairstylist. Grandma had always used the "bowl" technique for cutting her son's hair. Honestly, a bowl of some size would be placed on top of the kids head and Grandma would cut whatever stuck out. Efficient, but not necessarily attractive in all cases. Ma figured out how to comb, lift, and produce a product that looked nice.

There was one point during the late 1960's when long hair was the only style for boys that I objected to her hair cutting process. Why couldn't I let my locks brush my shoulders? Mom didn't think that was a good idea at all. She honestly countered with "If God wanted boys to have long hair, He wouldn't have let scissors be invented." I didn't buy into her logic, or ask why Jesus is depicted with over the shoulder length growth. Some arguments are just not worth having, God bless her.

Still, Ma passed the torch to the next generation. She even showed my wife, Babe, how to cut my hair during the summer of 1986. I never had to leave my house to pay for a trim again.

That summer of 1986 insert actually refers to the Fourth of July. Babe and I were celebrating a holiday break at the farm. Thinking about celebrations, there were always occasions to enjoy. Mom always had a birthday cake and a present for whomever turned a year older. With ten people in the house, rarely a month would go by without a sweetcake. She made sure we recognized other holidays as well.

As with any other family, there are lots of Christmas stories to tell. I'll try to restrain myself. Still, in the 1960's and into the 1970's, mom's kids and grandkids would gather at the family farm to exchange gifts and celebrate a bit. The presents really don't matter after all of these years still, mom made sure everyone got at least one thoughtful present even if they had moved out on their own. The gatherings were always something to look forward to in my youth. The original ten member family would at least double in size for that day as more offspring were added. One thing was for sure—there was always a glass or three of wine consumed. We needed to do something to relax the nerves in the large and crowded home.

There was one particular Christmas year that I do and don't remember. I do remember that during the late afternoon of Christmas eve, my parents and I drove the twenty five miles to the big town of that time for last minute shopping. Our last stop was at a very large warehouse club to get some most important groceries needed for the upcoming feast. We were a half an hour late. The store was closed. We were turned away without the "important" stuff. I do remember that our family dinner and celebration was a thrilling success. I don't have any idea of what food we might not have been able to purchase on the preceding day. Sometimes spirit is more nutritious.

Especially with a glass of wine in hand. Wine glasses were often refilled.

With Christmas in Minnesota, a person can only expect that weather would play a factor. One time, the whole family was huddled around the six PM news, checking which roads were closed, where the most snow was expected, which the wind was blowing and such. I had to pipe up and say something about just being thrilled by the family actually getting together given the wintry worries. The pretween in I spoke at the wrong time. One of my bossiest brothers slapped me across the face for interrupting the important forecast. It was a highly emotional setback for me. I pray that sometime he tries that again. Vindictiveness can run both ways. I suppose it could be expected.

Around 1960, mom started working with the Stanley Home Products company. Think about this as a cross of products between Avon and Tupperware. She became a remarkably good salesperson during the evening and an occasional afternoon get together of ladies sharing coffee and conversation. Soon enough she became a district manager in our county area and helped out other ladies who became employed by the same company. It's not like she had a thriving store and a warehouse full of supply. Mom just did very well. As one of my sisters put it "before mom started working we didn't have anything." She said it, not me. I'm just glad that Ma had another outlet for her wonderful personality even if it added an extra hour a week for me to sit in the car while she delivered goods to one of her hostesses.

On the wall in mom's basement Stanley storage room, she had placed a plague with her motto. It read something like "Count the day lost when the setting sun sees no good work by my hand done." She certainly lived up to that motto. It was many years later that my mom confided in me that there had been a couple of times during her life that she and dad had almost lost the farm. It certainly was not because of over spending. They fixed the situation by another refinance and one hell of a lot of work.

I only was exposed to one of the refinancing situations one time on a summer day. A couple of bank representatives were to visit the farm to check things out when I was about ten or twelve. I told Dad that we should get cleaned up, put on our best clothes, and wait in the house for this meeting. Dad would have none of that. He insisted that it would look better for us to be working when the bankers showed up. We grabbed a couple of paint brushes and started repainting the well house bright red. I had to keep painting while Pa talked to the bankers when they showed up.

It's ironic that we had to make work for that day. As if we didn't work most of the time anyway.

And, Stanley Home Products was good to me in another way. They had yearly competitions for employee's children to gain college scholarships. I scored highly enough on college entrance exams that I was rewarded by free tuition and books for my first year of college. Not bad for a farm boy. My immediately older sister scored higher a few years earlier. She pulled in more scholarship money than I, but she went to a private college instead of the public one I attended so I suppose we came out about the same expense wise.

During the winter of 1971 - 1972, mom and dad started going to Arizona to escape the blizzards. I guess they had to wait that long to make sure I had graduated from high school and was implanted into a college. I won't tell you about the parties I had in the farmhouse with college friends while the folks were gone. Mom and Dad had had teenage kids for nearly thirty years. I'd get a talking to upon their return in the spring. The next year I'd pull the same dirty trick. Some things are learned to be expected.

In the summer of 1976, I couldn't wait to bring my sweetheart to meet mom. My "Babe" commented later that she had never met her boyfriend's parents so early in a relationship. I guess we had been on at least two dates before the meeting. I knew how to pick'em though. By Thanksgiving, we received Mom's blessing to be married. I always looked at it this way. I had given the best mom the best daughter in law she could ever wish for. I had given the best wife the best mother in law she could ever hope for. I guess I got lucky on both accounts.

So, mom kept up with dad and had a bunch of golden years dabbling with Stanley products, farming during the good weather, and a trip south four months out of the year. This chapter could ramble on for another one hundred pages. They wouldn't be enough to pay homage to one of the best ladies that ever walked the face of this earth. In the end, we all just fade away. But in the minds of her children and grandchildren, she never will. Let's just leave it like that for now.

CHAPTER SIX
1953

That must have been an interesting year in the Harold and Edna Dobie household. After having three boys and three girls, I may have been an oops child. I was born on August 16th, about two weeks after my due date. Mom and the doctors had to do some finagling to get me into the world. Mom would never elaborate on the details though it did seem to be a risky delivery for the both of us. Glad we both made it.

To the best of my recollection, it was around or during the year 1953 that other changes occurred. In no particular order, indoor plumbing was installed which meant no more trips to the outhouse. The first family television was purchased. Somewhere along the line the family acquired a 1953 Chevrolet pickup truck. Growing up with all of these new state of the art, high tech devices, I was considered to be a "spoiled" child.

On the southwest side of the main floor of the farmhouse, there must have been a large, walk-in pantry about six feet by six feet which was transformed by the indoor plumbing. I grew up with a large bathtub (no shower), a toilet stool, and a small pedestal sink. Some kind of light brown four inch tile had been placed to a height of about three feet from the floor. The rest of the walls were painted a "shell white" color. Above the sink was a chrome covered metal medicine cabinet with a mirror which was about 16 inches both wide and tall. There was a wooden cabinet above the stool that sufficed for a towel storage. A couple of towel racks finished the project. There was no need for a shower curtain—no shower, just the tub for the kids to take their Saturday night baths in, two or more kids at a time washing up until one of them peed in the tub.

Always a Saturday night bath. The kids had to be clean for church on Sunday.

Yes, mom, dad, seven kids, and grandma equals ten people in a five bedroom house with one bathroom. Grandma helped us by having her own, personal chamber pot in her room. The male members of the family helped out by stepping behind a shed or tree to take a whiz after the chores were done before entering the house. This was less common during the summer months. During hot days we'd sweat out any excess water more. There wasn't a lot left over to whiz.

Luckily, I didn't have to deal with an outhouse except at the county fairgrounds and one of my Aunt's homes. I spent what seemed like a year there one week while my parents went on a trip. My aunt even gave me a taste of what I had missed out on in my spoiled youth. Saturday night I received a washing in a galvanized tub in the middle of her kitchen floor. She heated water on the stove and poured both the water and the kid into the tub. Needless to say I was very happy when my folks came to pick me up. Aunt didn't have any kids my age for me to play with anyway.

This was just one of a few occasions that my folks actually took a trip without me. I must have been whiney enough that they needed a break from. I'd get farmed out to a neighbor family or two for a few days at a time every few years. Can't say that I blame my parents. I'm still a brat.

Oops, I digress. Back to the 1953 chapter.

The television was about a two-foot by two-foot by two-foot wooden cube that was supported by four twelve-inch either metal or wooden legs. Basically, the viewers had to look down to see the show on the 19 diagonal inch black and white screen. That setup was quite common at the time. What was uncommon was the viewing selections.

Although we had the highest antenna on top of our house in the whole neighborhood, the Dobie family television only received one channel. That was KGLO from Mason City, Iowa, the CBS affiliate on channel 3. Any news, weather, sports, movies, or shows we watched were on that channel. Of course, the situation improved somewhat around 1960 when KEYC television from Mankato, MN came onto the airwaves. Yes, that was, and still is, channel 12. I think the two aforementioned stations probably had some financial ties. Either way, both of them were CBS stations. We didn't gain any new shows other than local newscasts.

Mom commented more than once that before the television came around, the living room chairs all faced one another. That made it easier to make eye contact and hold conversations. Once the TV was installed, the chairs all faced it. Fewer conversations. One sided communication.

The old black and white survived over a decade before it was replaced with a television that could receive in color. AND it even came with a remote control. The remote used a high pitched sound signaling system to quite literally move the mechanical circular channel selector to pull in stations. Being a young teenager, I was intrigued by this, especially when I found an old squeeze me toy that I could blow on at a pitch that would turn the television on and off and even increase the TV volume. My parents didn't like my innovation.

And yes, I said channels, not just channel 12. If there was just enough cloud cover and the wind blew from just the right direction the television would pull in KAAL, an ABC affiliate from the Austin - Albert Lea MN area, channel 6. On even more rare occasions, we'd be able to view KROC, channel 10 from Rochester, MN to see NBC shows. That didn't happen very often. Usually we'd view the CBS lineup which seemed dedicated to the 1960's hillbilly shows. Don't get me wrong, I still enjoy the small town, down home, feel good reruns of Andy Griffith and Petticoat Junction era.

One television rule was ingrained upon the children at an early age. We literally had to physically turn a dial on the TV to change the channel. The phrase "don't touch that dial" took on new meaning. If a person bumped the channel selector just a bit, it would mess up the reception. When it came to electronics, we were told not to mess with things. Perhaps that explains why people, such as myself, are not too savvy with computers and other new technologies. Touching the dial could mean breaking the machine.

And then there was the 1953 Chevrolet pickup. It was around a 4,000 pound vehicle made mostly of steel. Rounded fenders and all, painted almost an army green, it showed the flecks of Minnesota rust and dust. Upon occasion, we would put what we called the "stock racks" on its box back end. They were made of two-inch thick lumber and stood about three or more feet high. The stock racks were used when there was livestock to transport. I don't remember if we ever had to haul a cow, but I know the backend was filled with ten or twelve pigs from time to time. I wasn't even old enough to be in school yet when my parents transported some hogs to market at (I believe) Austin, MN. The seventy-mile each way trip was long and smelly. Dad gave me heck when I barfed on the front seat. Mom just cleaned it up. Long trip.

The pickup came fully decked out in the style of the times. It had both heat and keys. The truck had a four-speed floor shifter. The lowest gear was called either "super low," or "granny gear," depending on who you talked to. That gear was used for driving across field stubble and could not exceed five miles per hour. It worked well for getting started moving with a heavy load of grain on it. Eventually I found out that I could rev the engine, pop the clutch, and squeal the tires when I drove it on tar roads. The local town constable didn't appreciate that part.

As for the heater, it worked when it wanted to and would take the chill out of the cab's interior although the riders never did get very warm. This had something to do with the lack of padding or insulation. The steel exterior of the truck was the same steel on its inside. There was no padding on the dash or anywhere else.

Power steering depended on how strong and how much power the driver's arms had. The same can be said about its power brakes. How hard could the driver push down with the right leg? Power windows worked as long as a person turned the cranks which lowered them. Likewise, the air conditioner was in definite proportion to how far open a person could get the windows and the speed at which the truck was traveling. In other words, the pickup didn't have any of those things.

There was no electronic fuel injection either. To start the engine when it was cold, a person would have to pump the footfeed a few times and pull out the "choke" knob on the dash. Once started, it was necessary to slowly push the choke back in until the engine was running smoothly. In any case, it was necessary to turn the key into the on position. Then the driver would make sure the transmission was in neutral before pushing a foot switch to actually engage the engine starter motor. This sounds like quite an operation to go through, but it all worked out.

The old green beast was powered by a 235 cubic inch, straight line six cylinder engine. It was about impossible to stall it out. The top speed must have reached near sixty miles-per-hour, but the truck was shaking by the time you hit fifty. I'm sure all seven of dad's kids tried to push it past the sixty mile per hour speed. Kids will be kids. I'm sure we all failed in our attempts. The 235 was a staple of the Chevrolet / GMC line of vehicles for many years. My dad eventually purchased a grain truck, with a box about fourteen long and seven feet wide which had the same engine. Again unstoppable.

For that matter, my second car was a 1961 Chevrolet Bel Aire. Same engine. Years later I told my wife how I used to drive the '61 Chevy on a wide open, little used blacktop highway to school at ninety-three miles-an-hour. When she questioned why that speed I had to explain to her that ninety-three miles-an-hour was all the faster it would go. Of course, none of these vehicles had seat belts. Either they weren't required or hadn't been invented yet. It's amazing so many people survived without them.

Anyway, after about 18 years of service to the Dobie family, and after having been driven by seven different children, I was the 17 year old one that got the blame for ruining the pickup truck's engine. Dad growled about things like that.

CHAPTER SEVEN
MOO

My father didn't really like milking cows. He did it just because it was a steady source of income. Crops and livestock could be sold when prices were high enough, but the monthly "milk check" was a way to help pay the monthly bills, especially the electricity bill. And, the family always had milk to drink or use in foods. Pasteurizing and homogenizing milk properly requires the milk to be both nearly boiled and nearly frozen. We skipped that process and simply brought in a gallon from the barn and placed it in the house refrigerator as needed. On more than one occasion, there was no cold milk for my breakfast cereal. Those times we'd make a quick trip to the barn. I ate my cereal drenched in warm milk then.

The higher the amount of butterfat in the milk, the more pay the farmer would receive. Straight from the cow, most of the butterfat level was around four percent although a couple of them reached five or six percent. A rotating metal cream separator had been used when my parents were young to make the butterfat rise to the top of a vat of milk. This could be ladled off and turned into either cream, butter, or cheese. It was a time consuming process that I never had to deal with. The cream separator at my parents farm had been moved out of the way to an unused place in one of our farm buildings. We bought our butter at the grocery store.

As was a common practice at the time when I attended grade school, there was always a time for a milk break to feed us starving youngsters around ten o'clock in the morning. Two students would dutifully go down to the cafeteria and return with the infamous individual waxy covered cartons of milk for the class. One percent butterfat. Compared to what I was used to drinking, it was like drinking white water as far as i was concerned. I had to get special permission to add a chocolate mix to it just to make it palatable.

Some teachers were not amused by this out of norm conduct on my part. I never did get used to the "skim" milk life.

As near as I can tell, the farm's barn stood for nearly one hundred years. It was upgraded from time to time. For example, either before I was born or sentient enough to know, the barn's wood framed ground floor had been either raised or replaced with concrete blocks. In any event, the barn sure got a lot of use during my lifetime. Just a little bit of work was involved.

If you search for a picture of a cow you may be surprised at the number of different breeds there are. One of my Iowa cousins had either Guernsey or Jersey cows. They were a medium shade of brown. Our barn had space for fifteen cows to be milked. These cows were Holsteins, mostly black with large white splotches although some were white with large black splotches. And they all had two blue eyes, with the exception of one we had. I'm still not sure if it was Dad or I that hit the poor animal's left eye with a prong from one of our pitchforks while we were doling out hay. Even with that, the cow found her way to the feed bunk wagon in the cow yard and her stall in the barn. Didn't hurt the milk. Still feel sorry for the cow. Long dead Holstein either way.

At some point in the later fall of the year, Pa would pay for the services of a bull to be placed in with the cows. Breeding took place. One very busy bull. The same bull would never again meet those cows to prevent inbreeding. Fifteen calves were born in late August or early September of the following year. That would be a very busy time of year as the last cutting of hay would need to be baled, corn silage would have to be harvested, and the soybean crops would be very close to maturation, but those are other stories.

Usually the cows would be decent enough to make it into the barn to drop their newborns. Occasionally, one would be born in the wooded grassland a quarter of a mile from the barn. Then, it would be up to father and son to usher the cow and calf to the farmyard. Sometimes the cow would go into mother protection mode and not want its offspring to be bothered by the humans who fed her. There were times that Pa would take a baseball bat along to knock some sense into her while I quickly grabbed the calf. I'd climb up onto the back of the tractor while dad drove. The cow would invariably follow its baby. It was interesting being cow-growled at by an eight hundred pound beast while trying to hold onto a wiggly calf and the bouncy tractor at the same time. Fear is a great motivator. I never let go of either one.

The barn had five doors in it. Seven-foot sliding doors were placed at both the north and south ends. On the east side a four-foot-wide doorway allowed the cows to come in when it was milking time. The southeast corner opened to a milk storage area, another four-foot door opening. The southwest corner had a similar four-footer that hooked up to the silo.

Being about forty-by-sixty feet, the structure had room for several different floor plan opportunities. Running down the length of the barn on the west side was an approximately four-foot walkway to allow humans access to the silo and haymow. These foods were good ways of enticing the cows to find their assigned places in the stanchion stalls which were about seven feet in length each and faced the west. To get into their stanchions, the cows would have to step over a concrete gutter about two feet in width and one foot deep that also ran the length of the stanchion area. Of course there was a gutter. Cows poo anywhere they want to. Cleaning it out was at least a twice a week job, Any farm kid could tell you that this was a job where a five tine long handled fork was used. The three tined forks were used to move hay to the front of the cows. Five tines worked better for scooping the poo and straw mixture.

Semi gross side note here. When the female cows were in their stanchions and needed to urinate, it was best that a person stand back several feet. Watch out when a cow lifts its tail. The stream would be about an inch thick, shoot out four feet, and probably around a half gallon of yellow urine would fly by. Just throw some straw over it, and shovel into the gutter. It would go out with the poo a little later. Really no big deal. Urine is sterile anyway when it first comes out. After sitting around for a day or three its not so clean anymore. In any event, it was destined to become liquid natural fertilizer.

Down the center of the barn, running north to south again, was about a fifteen foot walkway. The cows needed room to turn into their stanchions. The people needed room to carry full milk buckets to the milk room. The tractor and manure spreader needed room to be backed into the barn when cleaning out the pens.

Along the east side of the building there were four pens framed in by tube steel. There were two pens with about forty inch railings just to the south of the east entry door. This is where the calves were held. Just north of the east entry door were two pens that had six foot high railings. One of these was dedicated mostly to the visiting bull. The other was called a freshening pen and was used by whichever cow that dad figured would be birthing a calf soon. Of course the six-foot-tall pens were used for other purposes. As baby calves became bigger, some were moved to the taller pens to give them a little more wiggle room.

Outside of the east door to the barn was about a one-half acre fenced in cow yard where the cattle could congregate around the feed bunk wagon, the water trough, or just mill about a bit. I've got to add in a side note here. I knew where the fence line was for three reasons. First, I could see the four-foot-high woven wire. Second, there was more than one time that I accidentally brushed up against the top strand of wire, which was both barbed and electrified. This would be a shocking experience for either man or beast. Both would back off of it quickly.

Third, there was one of those really bad, windy, snowy winters when I was a mid teenage kid. The snow blew in past the trees that were supposed to act as a windbreak to the north of the farmyard. It had just a high enough moisture content that it froze very stiffly when a subzero arctic front followed it. The cattle were able to walk over the fence. The temperature didn't matter when the cows were getting out. After guiding them back inside of the invisible fence line, Dad grabbed two scoop shovels and handed me one. Together we dug out the fence line, scooping out a trench about four feet wide and the same deep, over one hundred feet in length. The cattle couldn't jump over it and were contained back into their cowyard. Pa and I didn't jump over it either. We were too cold and tired after a few hours of shoveling.

At one point during that shoveling event, one rather nasty, foul tempered, half grown steer feeder calf kept rushing at me, trying to exert its will over my efforts. There was nothing particularly mean or uncommon about my reaction to this. I just knocked the steer in the head with my shovel a few times until it got the hint.

Steer left me alone after that.

Other than extremely cold days, the cows would stay in their outdoor cow yard but would congregate near the east barn door around 5:00 AM or PM, it was milking time. The door would be opened and in would walk the fifteen milk cows. They each knew which stanchion they were destined for; a little silage topped by ground feed awaited them. They would munch while we closed the stanchions around their necks. The cows were quite tame and with stanchions closed, they could not back up though they could reach down with their muzzles to eat, or turn their heads to get a drink of water from each stalls drinking dish. Thankfully the drinking dishes were all installed by a plumber and would refill automatically. The food the cows ate had to be placed in front of them by Dad or the farm kid worker.

That's where the term "manger" comes in. The milk cows ate their supply of silage and ground feed in front of them from a slight indentation in the concrete floor. This would eventually be refilled with a good amount of hay to be chewed as they stood there. I always had difficulty picturing a blessed baby being born and bedded in such a place, but that's how the church song went. I'm not sure our cows would have approved.

Likewise, there was always copious amounts of hay available in front of the calf pens. We baled a lot of hay. It got eaten.

And then, the milking would begin. Pa would start off by washing off each of the cows teats with a clean rag and giving them a little squeeze to make sure the milk would come out of them. I was probably only three or four years old when I also decided to check the teat milk. I was giving one of them a squeeze one evening and the cow didn't take kindly to it. One back leg kick sent me bouncing and crying across the cement floor. It was a traumatic experience which could have been eased over by a quick hug and a few kind words. Dad didn't have either of them to sooth me. Instead, I got yelled at for upsetting the cow. No, I don't fear cattle, but to this day I have a great respect for their strength. It was a very rare time that I had to put a milking machine on a cow. I felt more comfortable carrying the full buckets to the safety of the milk room.

I've got to interject a side story here. There is an old saying something about 'no man has ever sunk so low as to actually like his brother in law.' In my opinion, they first might seem like brothers but, having had a half a dozen or so, at one time I determined they could be placed into categories such as 'wimp' or 'jerk.' I'm a brother-in-law to several people and they can place me in any category they want, I'm beyond caring about what they think of me.

The vindictiveness Pa had inherited showed up one particular time during an afternoon milking. When I was about ten, one of my brother-in-laws, a vindictive bully, got some hay bale twine string and tied me up with my face stuck into the calf pen. He poured milk over my face and the calves had a fun time licking it off. I didn't think it was funny at all. Pa didn't come to my rescue. He laughed. I was probably stuck there for a five minute hour before being released. I have no problem classifying that particular brother-in-law and would enjoy meeting up with him again, adult to adult.

Dad had two milking machines to keep track of and moved down the row of cows until each had given up its white glory. The milking machines were steel containers with four plastic tubes which were each hooked up to lightweight metal cylinders with rubber linings. Powered by an air compressor system, the cylinders would produce an alternating suction and rest stage which would pull on the teats for a couple of seconds, off and on for several minutes, and squirt the milk into the steel containers. When the milk stopped flowing, the teats would become smaller and the rubber would start to slide off of them. Rarely would they fall off, Dad was too quick and accustomed to the process to allow that. On occasion. either he or I would slide a loose one back onto a teat to make sure all of the available milk was extracted but, for the most part, Pa had it down to a science and kept up with the established routine.

Milking was about a one to one and a half hour job. After each cow was milked out, Dad would pour the contents of the steel containers into a thoroughly washed out two or three gallon bucket. Then he'd start the next cow. Either he or I would carry the bucket to the milk room where we would pour it into a large funnel that sat on top of a ten gallon milk can. A filter was placed into the bottom of the funnel to keep out most of the guck that inevitably accumulated in the maneuvers. When a ten gallon milk can was full, it would be moved into a large, front loading refrigerator and we'd start filling the next one, swapping a new filter into the funnel.

Ten gallons of milk could weigh up to one hundred pounds. This required a certain amount of finesse to place it into the cooler, some sliding, some turning, and then a last deadlift of six to eight inches into the cold space. A couple of times a week a milkman didn't deliver the milk as they would in town. He picked up the milk from the farm. Needless to say, a milk truck driver muscled up quickly. I honestly don't remember whether the milk was poured into a tank on the milk truck or if he just swapped out empty milk cans for full ones, probably the latter.

Of course, while all of this air compressor noisiness was going on there were calves to feed as well. For the first month or two of the calves' lives, dad would leave a little bit of milk in each cow. When the milking machines were put away, the calf door pen would be opened. The calves instinctively knew which black and white cow to call mom. They would trot over for a milk meal and bonding time. It was a thrill and a joy to watch. After a couple of months, the calves would take to some eating of hay, corn silage, and ground feed. But, they still needed their milk.

The milk they received then became powdered milk mixed with water. The calves would stick their heads between the vertical steel bars of their pens and drink right from two gallon galvanized steel buckets. There might have been a four inch rubberized plastic nipple attached to the side of the buckets in the beginning, again my memory fails me, but it didn't take long until they figured out how to lap their new liquid from the offered pails. A few months later the calves would all be on solid food only. Again, there were plumbed in galvanized automatic filled water dishes for them to drink from.

Did calves ever get sick? They are actually extremely healthy animals. One way to tell if a person ever grew up on a farm is to ask them what color calf scours brown is. Calf scours disease was a concern although it was rare and relatively quickly and easily cured. A true farm kid will vividly remember the color of the scours poo and could trace it back to the calf that needed help. it was just a different shade of brown as normal poo.

In all of the years that I was involved in the raising of calves there was only one unfortunate incident that no one had any control over. One of our calves, I don't know, three, four, a few more months old got its tongue caught either in a gate hinge or a gate lock. When it jerked its head back, the calf lost its tongue, the calf lost its ability to eat. Few things go to waste on the farm. We had the calf butchered. If you happen to go to a restaurant and order milk fed veal, you'll know how tender and flavorful the meat is. It's from a young cow. We felt guilty eating it, delicious or not.

During the winter months, the cattle would be kept in that half acre pen by the barn. I use the word cattle here as besides the milk cows, the calves would grow out of their barn bars and would be allowed into the pen as well. After a year or so of growing, one of the yearlings would be destined to become next year's family steaks, burger, roasts, and stew meat. Usually the other fourteen would be sold off to cattle buyers either for further feedlots or for slaughter. There were a few times when dad rented some woodland with a creek running through it near our home, some of the yearlings may have been allowed to forage there to add on extra weight. Again, a long time ago.

But still the fact remains that it gets cold in southern Minnesota in the wintertime. Below zero temperatures could be mitigated by a rather large, if you will, degree by having fifteen cows and fifteen calves inside a closed barn for a few days during a cold snap. The hay in the mow provided good insulation although the walls were still cold. The people involved still wore long johns and an extra coat but their hands were warm enough so they could work without gloves. I imagine the teats of the milk cows appreciated that. Needless to say, all doors remained closed.

During the nice months, the cattle were allowed to walk down what we called "the lane". This was a dirt path that divided the farm fields between north and south. With a number of steel fence posts and a little electrified wire, the cattle didn't push their boundaries much as they walked down to about a six or eight acre area of the farm that was bordered by Lura Lake on the east end of our land. This is where there was grass to graze on, trees to seek shade from any hot sunshine, and a mud bottomed lake to drink from. When it got to around five in the afternoon, Pa would holler "come boss, come boss" and the cows would wander back up from the pasture for a meal and a milking.

As I remember it, during the 1950's and early 1960's our fields all had fences around them. If the weather held out decently for a few weeks after the fall harvest, the cows would be allowed to walk through these fields to forage whatever cobbed corn may have fallen on the ground by mistake, chew on the remnants of corn stubble that hadn't been plowed under; they found a new place to forage. Still, one good "come boss" was all that was needed to retrieve them. By the late 1960's the fence wire and most of the posts were removed. This allowed for an extra row or two of cash crop to be planted. It probably doesn't seem like much, but when there is an extra ear of corn every foot for a quarter mile field, it amounts to quite a bit of increased yield.

I've written just a bit about cow meals earlier in this document. Sure, the cows fed us with milk and meat. But, first we had to feed the cows. The staple of cow food were silage, ground feed, and hay. We'll take a look at silage first.

As mentioned before, there was an eight-foot by eight-foot room on the southwest side of the barn that crowded up against the silo. Silage, silo, it makes sense. Silage was nearly mature corn that was chopped up into small, inch square pieces, a mixture of brown and green stuff that could give off some obnoxious fumes. Spontaneous combustion? We just got lucky. The silo was thirty-feet-tall and about ten or twelve feet in diameter. A person would have to climb straight up a metal runged ladder, carrying a silage fork the entire way. Silage forks, attached to three-foot wooden handles, are about two-feet wide with steel tongs that stick out twelve to fifteen inches. And, there are a lot of tongs to make sure the inch sized silage shapes didn't fall through while a person was trying to pitch it down to the ground floor.

Oh yeah, the silage was heavy. Harvested while it was still green, there was a lot of moisture content involved. I'm guessing that each forkful weighed around twenty pounds. It took between fifty and one hundred fork fulls to obtain enough silage for the cattle. This would be tossed down the rib steel encased chute that the aforementioned steel ladder was attached to. That was phase one.

The second and third phases worked together so closely that I'll describe them at the same time. Again the silage would be forked, this time onto a cart that was around four feet long, two feet wide, and three feet deep. This cart would be filled about one third of the way up, then pushed around the corner into the barn and a forkfull would be deposited in front of each of the fifteen cow stanchions. That was the easy part.

Phase four of the silage saga again amounted to forking. Somehow during that hour or hour and a half long milking process, Pa would find time to load our feed bunk wagon as well. The bunk wagon was about four-feet wide, one-foot deep, and maybe fourteen-feet long. Dad would fill it with silage. This was the toughest scoop of all as the wagon stood off of the ground close to three feet. I know that others including me got in on some of this loading process but it was pretty much all of dad's territory. He had an incredibly strong back.

I'm sure some silage may also have found its way to the calves, I'm just not sure at what age they could digest it. Nor am I sure how much they got or how it got there. I guess I could have left this paragraph out.

Every other Saturday, or sooner if the need existed, we would have to grind feed. There was a granary building about thirty feet square where shelled corn and oats were stored inside of wooden bins. Just inside the granary there was an open area and in it sat a metal feed grinder, probably three feet wide, three feet high, and four feet long. It had a one foot steel wheel attached to it to turn the grinder and mix the feed. Dad would drive a tractor front first near the granary and we would attach a long, one foot wide heavy duty rubber belt to the mixer's wheel and to a similar wheel that was part of the power take off of the tractor. Backing up slightly to tighten up the belt, the fun and games would begin.

By removing one of the granary's wooden slats, corn would either pour out or could be shoveled out. The same was true for the bin of oats. And there was always a bag of feed minerals that we would get from town to add into the mix. Turning on the tractor power take off, the mixer would begin rotating. There were formulas as to what the mixture should be. Maybe four scoop shovels of corn, one of oats, and a cup container of premixed minerals. Something like that. The ground feed produced would fall onto the floor of the granary. After an hour or so of this work, enough would be produced for the coming week or weeks. Why do I place this process into the silage story? Well, it's part of the big picture.

First, one of my older sisters and I would drive a tractor out into the cattle lot while dad was milking. We'd hook it up to the feed bunk wagon. Another sister would open and close a gate to allow us access without any of the feeder calves to make an unwanted exit. Tractor driving sister showed me how to maneuver the machine when I was about nine years old, just before she headed off to college. After that, it was all on me.

I'd pull the wagon by the silo room exterior entrance door where Pa would usually be the one to fork the silage on. After that, I'd pull the wagon over alongside the sliding granary door and start covering it with ground feed. Sometimes a little extra mineral substance would be sprinkled on over the top of the feed. Then it was tractor time again and the wagon would be pulled back out into the cattle lot with a gate guard on duty. Once unhitched, I'd drive the tractor back into the machine shed. Tractor driving sister had shown me how to rev the engine a few times before shutting it down. That way an exciting and rewardingly loud backfire would occur. Just another one of life's little perks. And the whole process was completed just in time for dad to let the milk cows out of the barn so they could indulge themselves from bunk wagon goodness.

I got a little bit ahead of myself while describing the silage and ground feed. At some point during the milking process, I'd find myself and whomever else might be around going up the ladder into the hay mow. Usually at least three or four bales of hay would need to be thrown down, as well as a bale or two of straw for bedding. The amount depended on the time of the year. During the summer, the cattle would get quite a bit of green food foraging in the pasture by the lake. In winter months, an extra bale or two of hay might be needed to keep them healthy and well fed. Winter months in southern Minnesota meant it was dark by five PM. I'd be up in a hay loft with a couple of dozen cooing pigeons with only one, one hundred watt light bulb to show me the way. Sometimes a person might find this a little spooky.

Of course my five or six-year-old nephews and nieces would have to hang out with young teenager Uncle Dennis if they were visiting during chore time. A trip to the haymow was always included. Once, after enough hay bales had been dropped down through the sliding door opening, I couldn't find a niece that had followed me up the ladder. Eventually I heard what sounded like a whimper and tracked it down. There was the wayward four year old who had slipped in a gap between bales. She was half crying and plenty shook up. I just pulled her up and out and told her she was just acting like a gopher in a gopher hole. With a hug and a few kind words, the tears turned into smiles.

Were there times when a tweenager would try to skip out on work? What do you think? Only once did dad really raise a fuss about it. I had been stuck in town after a parade or some function one day and the folks were running late, like two hours late. When I finally got a ride home I was more than just a little miffed. Grabbing my bike, I headed off down our gravel road and intentionally missed the evening milking chores. Pa was not amused. Dad had a temper and used it for cussing us kids out probably too often, but that night I got slapped up the side of the head once, and only once. I ducked the second hand and ran upstairs. Remember, Pa was probably pushing sixty years old by that time, with knees that had experienced too much jumping. He didn't follow me up. Can't say I blame him for either of these things.

Our moods were quite chilly towards one another for a time after that.

Some things just work out the way they do or are destined to be. Dad had been milking cows basically since he was able to walk. As he neared his sixtieth birthday he had had enough. Pa was having difficulty training a new cow to take the milking machine. One of his best cows had accidentally stepped on one of its teats rendering it a very difficult milking situation. One day he just walked into the house after the morning milking and told Ma that he was done with milk cows. By that time the five oldest children were living independently, one was in college, and I was nearing driver's license age. I think he could see his free help was about used up.

So, the milk cows were sold. Dad bought a couple of dozen head of feeder cattle instead. That only lasted a few years. There was no need for the lane or the pasture anymore, just a feeding area by the barn. The pasture was cleared of trees by a bulldozer. Late one fall night, he and I went down to the grassy area that was left with a couple of gallons of gas and some matches. With the west wind to our back, plowed ground all around us, and the lake to the east we produced a six acre fire that got the attention of a couple of neighbors. No harm was done. A few days later, Pa plowed up the virgin ground. After about a week's worth of work of us clearing stones, some as big as a pillow, he extended his crop land.

Why did the feeder cattle only last a few years? The feeder cattle liked to hunker down inside the barn during the winter months. Needless to say, they left a mess of feces. Like two or three feet thick from one end of the barn to the other. It took days of forking to remove it. We couldn't get a tractor bucket into the barn, the barn ceiling was just too low. Another reason to quit cows altogether was that I definitely had my driver's license and was heading off for college soon. Again, there goes another worker. And I was the youngest, therefore the last kid worker. Finally, Pa and Ma decided that they had had enough of Minnesota's winters. Like many of our farm neighbors, they purchased a trailer house in Arizona and spent their cold season down there.

Years later, a friend got after me about not being very worldly. I didn't have the traveling experiences that my friend had. It was true. We didn't travel very much or very far or for very long. Cows didn't take weekends off. They still needed their twice a day milking. Hiring a neighbor to take over for a day or two didn't happen very often. Usually, we'd have to be home around five or six in the afternoon for chores. Not much of a traveler at all. Not very worldly either. Wouldn't have it any other way.

And the barn, well it couldn't just sit empty. Dad kept seven sows and their piglets there. I'd come home occasionally on weekends to help out, but most of the winter barn hog raising fell onto one of my brothers who farmed a couple of miles away. A couple of years later even the pigs went away. The hog story will be another chapter. And so the barn sat empty and in need of paint and repairs. Another chapter.

CHAPTER EIGHT
OINK

The hog house had been placed on the east side of the farm yard. It was another one of those wood framed buildings, about twenty-five feet wide and thirty-five feet long. The walls were eight-feet high. Naturally, it had an attic hayloft mostly filled by bales of straw for insulation or occasionally a back up plan if necessary for livestock bedding, just in case the barn's supply ran low. Mostly, the attic mow just gathered a lot of dust. There was a three foot hinged human door on both the east and west ends along with a couple of windows, set up high enough so the pigs couldn't get to them, for ventilation on warm days.

Several windows allowed light to shine in on the south side of the building. Also on the south side were two, vertical slide doors that could be closed and opened only by humans when necessary. It was rarely necessary. Farmers of that era wanted the pigs to have access to the outside as much as possible. That meant less pig poo in the building to fork out.

The building's floor was concrete, straw was laid out on top of it, pigs nestled into it for sleeping. And they pooed there too. Farmer dad and mostly the sons would enter the building through the west door. Straight ahead of the door was about a four-foot fenced-in walkway for people to walk unimpeded by the swine. There was a pen on the north side and one on the south. The people walkway ended about four feet from the east end of the hoghouse so the pigs could walk from one side to the other. Rudimentary but nonetheless ingenious wooden fence panels could be lifted, moved, and placed to restrict the hogs living area when necessity arose.

When I was a young child, the pigs had access to about a twenty-foot by twenty-foot concrete slab when they left the hoghouse. This opened up into about a two or three acre fenced in wooded area that worked its way around the south side of the farmyard. The trees in this hog pen took a beating from the rub up a side swine but still provided somewhat of a southern windbreak for the farm's building site. I thought it was a good idea to have that breeze stopper area but Pa decided he could better use the land for crops. So, the trees were cut down, stumps were bulldozed out, and cropland eventually conquered.

There was another reason to confine the hogs into a smaller space. Once in a while, a sow would deliver her ten or so baby pigs near a tree instead of her designated hoghouse stall. Mothers always take great offense when they perceive a threat to their offspring. Moving mom hog and baby pigs required a great deal of fitness and bravery by their human owners. It was best done by several men with scoop shovels to guide the large creature as piglets were loaded into a tractor pulled wagon and wee, wee, wee'd all the way to the sow's stall in the hoghouse. Mother pig always chased after their babies' calls. Mother pig always outweighed a full grown human by at least two to one. Mother pig was always aggressive.

At some point in the late 1960's, what little of the hog yard was completely done away with. That was when a concrete feeding floor was poured. A half a dozen local farmers helped spread, level, and trowel an area of about fifty feet by fifty feet. The farmers were all going to that kind of model at the time and helped each other out as they each contrived their own feeding floor. Posts were set, fence wire was stretched, and two fourteen foot long gates were attached. One gate was on the southwest corner, another on the north east. A line of posts and fence was maneuvered in the middle running north and south. A gate was attached to it as well. This sufficed to keep different age pigs apart when needed.

About once a year, some pig would bump into the southwest gate just the right way to unhook it and the hogs would soon be wandering over the farmyard. Ma, pa, I, and whomever else was around would then have to form a loose circle around the wayward swine, wave our arms around, talk loudly to the animals, and herd them back to the feeding floor. This task was actually easier than a person would think. The feeder pigs would rarely be over two hundred pounds each and seemed to enjoy the attention they were receiving. We never lost a hog. We'd just tighten another piece of chain to the gate, then wait until next year's event.

Yorkshire or some other breed of white hogs were the kind which were raised on my family's farm. Dad always kept about seven sows around. Each one had a wood sided stall on the north side of the hoghouse which they were kept in at night. It didn't take too long for each sow to be trained as to which pen was theirs. Around twice a year, the two sides of the feeding floor would be separated by the aforementioned gate and it was rent-a-boar time. A few months later, the sows would deliver about ten to twelve piglets each, usually in the confines of their stalls. Once in a while a sow would give birth on the feeding floor and we'd have to convince it to go back to the proper stall. That usually meant grabbing a newborn, giving it a squeeze to make a sound, and then run to the hoghouse. Mama pigs were again aggressive and protective of their babies. It was always an interesting race.

So, there were always seventy plus swine on the property. The baby pigs would turn into feeder pigs and be kept around for a year or so to gain enough weight to be sold to a slaughter house. There was always at least one of them that made it into our huge basement chest freezer as well.

Hogs needed to eat to gain weight. The seven sows were actually fun to feed. Every morning and afternoon we would let them out of their stalls and get them onto the feeding floor. There was the feeding trough. The feeding trough we used was constructed of wood. Two fourteen-foot long, two-by-twelve planks were nailed together in the form of a V. These were supported by three foot long two by twelves on each end to keep the top of the V upright and stable. A bunch of scoops or a bushel basket of ground corn feed would be spread the length of the feeding trough.

The sows didn't pay much attention to it until we'd run a hose or pour water buckets on top. Then, the mama pigs noses would dive straight in. If you ever wanted to know where the term "slop the hogs" came from, this is a brief but accurate example. At the end of the feeding time there would not be a single piece of grain or drop of water left. After a half-an-hour of stretch-break/walk-around-the-feeding-floor time, the sows were then herded back to their stalls.

During the early 1960's, Dad had an auger wagon. This was a metal, four sided contraption with a tube enclosed screw type auger attached to the back end of it. We would scoop ground up corn and oats from the granary, throw it into the auger wagon, and tractor drive it onto the hog feeding floor. The auger would then be employed to lift the feed above a six-foot-high, six-foot-diameter metal cylinder hog feeder. The covered feeder cylinder was surrounded by a group of trays with metal lids on them. When a feeder pig got hungry, the feeder pig would lift a lid and eat. Gravity refilled the feeding tray. For about a week. It seems like Saturday was the best day to refill the hog feeder. It may have had something to do with Saturday not being a day of school, so I was around to help.

In the late 1960's Pa finally got around to buying a machine that would both grind, mix, and auger the feed. Before that we would have to hook up a tractor to the granary's steel and iron feed grinder, and then start scooping corn and oats into it. Once enough feed was ground, we'd have to scoop it again into the auger wagon. The tractor pulled feed grinder was a big step up. One less ton of scooping was involved. I loved that new technology.

Besides eating feed, pigs needed water. This was accomplished with two mechanically controlled water dishes. If pig needed water, pig would push snout onto a metal plate at the bottom of the dish and water would fill up dish. Pig got water. Most of the time. There is such a thing as called winter in southern Minnesota and on a few subzero days, a water dish might freeze up. That's when dad would send me to the house to fetch a gallon of hot water. Between pouring and prodding, the dish would warm up enough to become operative again. Most of these freeze up times would be discovered at the end of chore time, somewhere near six PM. The sun set around five PM. We were cold and working mostly by flashlight and feel.

Sending the hogs to market was always an exciting day. A large, high-sided truck or two would back up near the hog house and run a walled ramp into its door. Sending seventy, two-hundred-pound pigs into a narrow chute met with some swine complaining. There was a good deal of man power involved in the push. In an open area, a person can guide a pig from one place to another with a scoop shovel. If you want to turn the hog to the left, you place the scoop near the right side of its head. The opposite is true if you want to turn it to the right. A shovel placed directly in front of a pig's eyes would usually make it stop. Shovels were used on market days as well, however three-foot-wide metal hog panels were also employed.

A few of the truckers used electrified hog zapper sticks to achieve their means. Nothing like getting a few volt amps on the rear end to make an animal move forward. For the rest of us, we just kept pushing the herd forward. We never let one get away.

Before, during, and especially after the sell off, there would be many poo days. It seemed to me that these were also often on Saturdays although I know dad cleaned stuff up most of the time without me. Some of the poo could be forked out the south side slide up doors onto the feeding floor, but most of it went through the human sized east and west doors. The tractor would back up the manure spreader wagon and the game was on. Pa never approved of the kind of music I liked and, for that matter, there was no radio in the hoghouse, so we mostly worked in the quiet solitude of our thoughts. After a few hours the deed would be done and fresh straw would be placed on the floor. The hoghouse would be good for a couple of more weeks.

The feeding floor cleaning was actually the fun part. We'd shoo all of the hogs to one side or the other of the divided area and close the gate on them, then clean out one side at a time, moving pigs as necessary. Dad had a scoop bucket he could hook up to the front of one of the tractors. It would pick up a bunch of goo every time he moved it forward, towards the building. With the manure spreader placed at the south end of the feeding floor, the tractor bucket would just reach over the fence and dump the waste straight in. There was inevitably some poo that got pushed up against the hoghouse and had to be forked or shoveled into the bucket but that's what the kid was for. And again, the manure would be spread over the fields during the winter or onto the alfalfa area during the summer.

Once Pa had finally sold off the cattle around 1971, the sows were moved into the barn. That gave a lot more room for the growing feeder pigs in the hoghouse and on the feeding floor. In the barn, horizontal metal tubed stalls were placed for the mama pigs to give birth and nurse their young. When it came around time for the little ones to be delivered, we'd squeeze a hog's teat nipple to see if any milk was being produced. If we saw milk, we knew it was delivery day. The test never failed.

Mother pigs still had to be let out twice a day for their slopping meal. In their steel tube barred stalls, the hogs would go in head first. At the back of a steel stall, there would be a metal panel to unlatch at the top, and then lift up out of a couple of retaining hooks at the bottom. This maneuver needed to be done pretty much in one motion. Mama hogs were eager to stretch their legs and get a meal.

Sometimes the mothers back legs would be too quick for us and we'd just have to drop the back panel. They'd rapidly move backwards over it. Once, and only once was I not speedy enough. Either Mrs. Pig was too fast or I was too slow. Basically smashed the big toe on my right foot. No bones were broken, but I lost the toenail. After a couple of weeks of complaining, Ma took me to the doctor. He told me he wasn't going to touch it, just look at it with his forceps. One quick jerk removed the remnants. I said "Ow!" On the way home, I said a few other things.

It happened that a stillborn baby pig would be pushed out along with the healthy ones. It also happened that a malformed, skinny little runt which was destined to not survive would arrive into the world. Using a cement block as a pedestal and a hammer for a utensil, there would be a quick death blow delivered upon the occasional runt of the litter. It wasn't a matter of animal cruelty, it was part of the nature of the business. Times being what they were, no rendering truck was called to deal with such a small dead animal. They were just thrown into the manure spreader and disposed of with the next load of poo.

So was the life cycle of an oink described. However, I left out one important part for the end. This part might seem a bit testy to you, double entendre intended. Half of the seventy piglets would be female. In other words, leave them alone, they'll grow, gain weight, and be shipped off when their time was due. The other half of the young pigs would be male. Male pigs have a tendency to be a little more aggressive and enjoyed the natural instinct for breeding. Something had to be done to avoid both of these things.

A couple of months after their birth, it would be castrating day. Again, a few farmers in the area would trade help when that time came. Again, I was part of the package deal with my much older father. After separating the boy pigs from the girl pigs, one of our neighbors who was very handy with a surgical blade would do the actual cutting. Dad and I and whomever else was around would do the holding.

You don't just sneak up behind a boy pig and make a knife swing. A person like me would walk straight up towards the front of the around twenty or thirty pound piggy, grab him by the back legs, lock my feet around his front legs, and lift. It was preferable to have my back up against a wall or fence. This would expose the testicles of the soon to be neutered oink. That's where the surgical steel blade handy man would do his part of the duty. There would be a couple of deft, quick flicks of the blade and the job was done. I would always sigh with relief after each pig I was holding had been successfully dealt with. Holding a pig in such a manner placed my own groin area very close to the part of the pig that was being removed. I'm glad neighbor had a sure hand. I didn't feel like going through an ordeal like that on my human body parts.

As I've noted before, again and again, labor was traded off between farmers. I was part of the package deal with my dad. Between our farm and neighboring farms, I must have held up hundreds, if not thousands of young male pigs for neutering. It was expected.

There was only one time when we tried to remove the testicles from a small pig that was just a little too young. That was the only time I saw any bleeding. Otherwise, the neutered boy pigs just ate, drank, and carried on much as they had before the slicing. It didn't seem to bother Dad or the neighbor. Pa just held the pig upside down and let our neighbor drive the '53 Chevy pickup into town for a quick stitch up by the local veterinarian. That was successful too. So did we end up with a pile of testicles to throw on the manure spreader? Nope. Toss them over the fence to the sows and growing hogs. Pigs will eat just about everything. Very little gets wasted on a farm.

Oink's about done. I need to veer off on a related moo story. There was one time during my late teens that Pa had promised to spend an evening over at neighbor Bob's farm. By that time, Dad was nearly sixty and was tired out after a day of farm work. That was no problem, I'd just go over instead. Again, it was a package deal.

Bob's summer evening's work was not to castrate pigs. It was a time to prevent boy cows from becoming bulls. In other words, steer up. Bob probably had fifteen or twenty, two-hundred-pound victims in mind. These we sorted into a holding pen and then, one by one, forced them up against a fence and used a gate to keep them trapped. I'm not sure who the gentlemen that performed the castration were. One would hold up the male cattle tail and force the tail flat against its back. The young bull wouldn't jump up much in such a position. The other fellow did the slicing and removing. These testicles were somewhere between golf ball and base ball size. Each pair was sealed inside a plastic bag and placed into a large cooler which was half full of ice. They didn't get thrown to the hogs. Their destiny was to become Rocky Mountain Oysters.

I never had a hankering for Rocky Mountain Oysters although I've seen them listed as gourmet cuisine on the menus of a few bars I've been in since then. Maybe a little alcohol would lead to a dare which would lead to a dish. Not me.

Bob actually asked me how much money he owed me for helping him out that evening. Of course I declined. Pa couldn't make it, I was just taking his place. It was expected. Besides that, the lesson I had learned was earnings enough for me.

To put this into further perspective, In my preteen years, Dad would kick me out of the barn whenever there was a new "moo" being born. I also had to exit during cutting off the cow horn times. Some things, he figured, were just a little too gross and somewhat bloody for a child to participate in.

So, that's a lot of oink with just a little moo too. Onto bigger and better things. Or smaller things that weren't all that much better.

CHAPTER NINE
CLUCK

Yup, that's one of the sounds a chicken makes. Put a couple of hundred together and that turns into a lot of clucks. Put them all together in a twenty-by-forty hen house and it turns into a high decibel cacophony of noise. And the opposite of cluck is uncluck. That's the sound of a chicken that is no longer in the living world. Perhaps this sounds like the beginning of a Stephen King novel. On our family farm it was just part of an expected process. We were in the business of raising food.

The hen house sat about one hundred feet straight south of the barn. The back, north wall was only about six-feet-high, the front eight. I believe the north wall was insulated with loose straw and had interior twelve inch planks nailed up on the inside as well. Two-by-fours angled down from the top of the north wall, out about six feet or so. Long two-by-two lumber was nailed into the angle boards at every two feet horizontally to give the chickens a place to roost. Chickens clutch on branches, or two by twos, and literally sleep while standing up off of the ground..

I was surprised to learn that my dad had actually built the hen house. I never thought of him being a carpenter. Some work just had to be done. One or two of my uncles got in on the project as well. One of these uncles worked for the post office in a nearby town. I hadn't figured him to be a carpenter either. Evidently, the hen house was built around 1940, again before my time. In my childhood, it had just always existed.

On the south wall it is best described as rows and rows of twelve-inch wooden square boxes in which the chickens laid their eggs. Perhaps you could think of it as sixty or so birdhouses without the peaked roofs set side by side, one on top of another. There were tip-in windows along the south side wall as well for ventilation during the warm months. They just didn't tip-in too far so the birds couldn't get out. Three-foot-wide human doors on the west, east, and south side provided access. Though these doors were solid, they also employed framed chicken wire doors to be used for ventilation as well during warm times. The chickens never left the building. The concrete floor was covered with corn cob pieces. These pieces were obtained whenever we used a sheller machine to remove corn kernels from our ear corn cribs. Nothing much was wasted on the farm.

The building had an attic that was filled with straw bales for insulation or to be used as an emergency supply of animal bedding if it was ever needed. It was rarely needed. I can only remember one time when the attic mow was ever emptied. That was when I was under the age of ten and was not allowed to assist. It seems some rats had decided to make it their dwelling.

Dad, my next door neighbor uncle, and my three older brothers, all in their mid to upper twenties, cleared out the old bales during one spring day. Armed with a variety of baseball bats, hoes, and pitchforks, and aided by the two farm dogs, the rat patrol took place after dark. As I was not allowed to join in the hunt, everything I'm placing here is based on reports from the frontline of the battle.

No humans were injured although the rats proved elusive and aggressive. The dogs seemed to relish the action. After being trained to be passive around people, they reveled in their chance to seek retribution on the nasty, long tailed, huge mouse creatures. I'm not sure how many rats were involved, but there must have been dozens killed. None could possibly have escaped the chasing dogs. Either the rats were disposed of in a fire or they went into the manure spreader and were scattered on the hay field. Again, that was a once in a lifetime encounter and a heck of a way to start a chapter about chickens. Stephen King, where are you?

Somewhere in the chicken growing process, probably during the month of April, the old chickens would be sold to a food packing plant. This was followed by scooping out the leftover corn cobs and an abundance of chicken poo. Again, the manure spreader came into play. After being cleaned up pretty well, in went the new corn cobs, along with around two hundred purchased yellow female chicks which were called "pullets."

We would crowd them in near the center of the chicken coop with walls of twelve inch planks. Long metal trays were placed in with them and needed to be filled with some kind of corn based chicken feed, along with a few inverted one gallon jugs of water for them to drink from. These both needed to be refilled at least twice a day, complete with rinsing out the water jug trays. Chickens aren't necessarily tidy, bits of dirt always found their way into the water trays. Above the chick area were hung at least a couple of heat bulbs with reflective covers. These were highly sought after on chilly days and nights.

It is inevitable that a few chicks would die of natural causes. Sometimes a leg would get stepped on and immobilize an unfortunate creature. Chicks could be almost human-like in aggression, and quite literally peck a downed sister to death. When an injured chick was found by a human, we would just crush them so it wouldn't suffer. More fertilizer for the hay field.

Pullets were highly sought after by farmers who were searching for egg producers, and had to be purchased. As with any other life form, about half of the eggs hatched would be male. These were not as valuable. Male chicks, called "cockerels" at times, could be obtained for free. Just buy fifty pounds of chicken feed, and get fifty cockerels. Dad would purchase one hundred pounds of feed. Pullets were for laying eggs. Cockerels, or rooster chicks, had a different destiny.

About fifty feet west of the north side of the barn was what we called a "brooder house." Maybe being fifteen-feet-long and ten-feet-wide, it was just over six-feet in height and was covered by a curved roof. Again, it had a few windows on the south side for light and ventilation, and a door on the east side to allow human access. This building had a wooden floor which sat up off of the ground about a foot high. Somehow I inherited the duty of cleaning out the structure, corn cobs, poo and all. I caught heck one year as I forgot to remove the tar paper that lined the floor and a ways up the walls. Back to work I went. This was followed by installing new tar paper and a new corn cob base.

The cockerel - rooster area became my domain pretty much because of me wanting to play softball. The only outlet for a softball playing farm kid, other than occasional neighborhood or farm family member work up games, was to join the 4H club. That way I could get to town every week or so and play on the 4H softball team. Keep in mind that as a young farm child eight miles from the nearest small town, getting a chance to leave the farm was at best once a week for a short shopping trip. Or to play softball. 4H members were required to have some kind of exhibit at the county fair. Roosters were my way to meet the requirement.

Whereas the main chicken house had a water hydrant plumbed into it, the brooder house did not. This meant that twice a day I would have to carry a half-full five gallon bucket of water and a half-full bucket of chicken feed a couple of hundred feet to meet their nutritional needs. Sixty-pound boy carrying two, twenty-pound buckets—it was expected. I shouldn't complain, this was just a May to September operation. The rooster's lifespans would come to an abrupt end on butchering day.

But, let's dwell on happier thoughts for a few moments. There were a few times when the baby chick roosters would be picked up before it was warm enough for them to survive in an unheated brooder house. On those rare years, they would live their first week or so of their lives in a boarded off area in the basement of the house, warmed by a heat lamp. It was always fun to see the little yellow creatures hopping about. Did they stink up the place? Not really. They were too small to emit too much poo. Plus, the farmyard always had some livestock smells. It was never as intense as the stench created by 21st century huge, crowded operations. In the 1960's, smaller smells just dissipated into the air.

The beautiful little yellow chicks, after a couple of weeks, lost their cute fuzziness and sprouted white feathers as they grew rapidly larger. By the summertime, the brooder house would be overcrowded. That's when the door would be opened and the roosters could venture outside. For the most part they stayed near their brooder home; they knew where their feed and water was located. Eventually, as they gained their limited hopping flight abilities, the white birds would find their way to the low branches of a grove of trees which lined the north side of the farmyard. Roosters clung or "roosted" on the branches. It was easiest to catch them at night.

Near the end of the nice weather summer days, the cockerel roosters would have grown pleasantly plump. After a check on the weather forecast and the amount of available help, a butchering day would be determined. The day would always have to be one that allowed for outside work.

By dusk on the evening before they were to meet their demise, tools of the trade would be in place. Crates built of slats of wood needed to be gathered. There were several of them. The crates were probably four feet in length, two-and-a-half feet in width, and one foot tall. There was a twelve inch square door on the top of each one that could be closed from the outside. Dad would bring out an old wood stump with two, four inch nails halfway pounded into it about a couple of inches apart. He would sharpen up the farm ax.

Each of the human participants would be armed with a "chicken hook," made up of a short wooden handle attached to some stiff wire that had a half inch hook at the end. Just as it started turning dark, the roosters would make one more stand on low tree branches. Reaching up with our chicken hooks, we would grab a rooster leg and pull down one flustering bird after another, stuffing them into the crates. No rooster ever completely escaped although some of the confused creatures tried valiantly. Fluttering wings and scrambling claws, we always got them all. And, that's where they spent their last night on this earth.

After the morning chores were completed and the humans fed, the day of butchery would begin. One by one, the roosters were taken from the crates. Pa was excellent at his task. Somehow he could manage to get both chicken legs, and both chicken wings in his left hand. With the neck of the bird placed and pulled firmly between the two stump nails, his right armed ax would deliver a severing blow. He'd have to let each one bleed out for a minute and stop their death throes, then hand the carcass to my sisters and I. We had the next step in the process, feather removal of the edible chicken remains. The family dogs took care of most of the lost heads. The rest either went to the manure spreader or to the hogs. Very little went to waste on the farm.

I had a small three-foot-long red wagon, the kind a kid gets to drag along behind their tricycle. Piled with the beheaded chickens, we'd pull it over to the barn and deep dip them one at a time into a vat of boiling hot water. Next, we would tie the dead bird's feet with twine string and hang them from nails in the barn ceiling. Then came, quite literally, the chicken plucking. Hot feathers would be pulled from each bird. Pulling off the feathers was best accomplished by starting at the leg area and rubbing the palm of a hand down, towards the remains of the chicken neck. We kind of had to work against the natural grain of the feathers for easiest removal. Dead, hot, wet chicken feathers are not pleasant to work with. The feathers would drop onto the floor, some shoveling into the manure spreader was required.

It was a task I never relished. It evidently was never a task I excelled at either. After delivering the nude roosters to the house for butchering, I'd usually receive a lecture that I hadn't done a good enough job. Whether it's poo or families, stuff flows down hill. Being the youngest and smallest at that time, I was in the valley.

The actual cutting apart of the birds took place in the large basement sink area. First though came the part called "singeing." I don't mean a tube was warbled, I mean the whole bird carcass was moved back and forth above a wide candle flame to singe off the small "pin feathers" which remained after the large white feathers had been removed. Following that, my mom and an older brother, and whomever else was skilled enough would use knives to separate the meat and unwanted portions. The meaty parts were rinsed off with water and ended up in the household's large chest freezer. Unwanted portions were placed in literally a "slop bucket". Either I or whomever was around would, yes, "slop" the hogs. Chicken guts went to help feed the pigs. Very little was wasted on the farm.

And so, the job would go on for the whole day. Dad would come and help with the basement butchering part after the beheadings, outside clean up, and tools put away tools were taken care of. By then it would be afternoon chore time. I'm not sure if we ate a chicken supper that day or not. I'm thinking probably not as chicken takes time to bake and we were pretty busy. We may have already had our "fill" of chickens for the day. Of course, it doesn't take long to fry chicken parts. Who knows, maybe yesterday's rooster was today's supper. One hundred roosters, even after doling out part of the day's work to help compensate the helpers, still left the farm family with a diet of at least one chicken meal every ten days, and it lasted for a whole year. At least I didn't have to carry buckets of food and water to them anymore.

Now, all of this might seem a gross and cruel way to get meat from chickens. I learned later from one of my aunts who worked in a chicken butchering facility that corporate ways may have been more expedient. Killing the chickens before butchering in a factory was done by using a sturdy needle, poked right through the poultry's eyes. What little brain a chicken might have would be between the eyes so, hopefully, the chicken felt no pain. Whether factory or farm, it is important to note that chickens weren't pets. They were grown for meat. Butchering was expected.

I've got to go back to my 4H story here. As noted before, roosters were my way into the softball games at the county fair. Dad would help me pick out the five fattest ones and mom would help me get them to the fair grounds to be placed into crates for judging. I'd usually receive a mediocre red ribbon, better than a poor white one, but not as good as a top notch blue ribbon. There was one year when our roosters were a brown hue instead of the leghorn white. Wouldn't you know it, they stuck out in the crowd and raised the attention of the judges. I received the grand champion purple ribbon award, the best roosters in the county raised by a young teenager.

Although most poultry, and especially roosters were not allowed to compete, I would have won my way to show my wares at the state fair. Instead, I, along with all the other grand champion winners got their names and categories in the local newspaper. I didn't make any big deal out of it and was glad that none of my school classmates read the article. It said "Dennis Dobie, champion cock

eral"

It's just the way the wrap around worked in the newspaper articles of the time. Some things never live up to the hype.

So much for the roosters; back to the hen house. By the end of the summer, the pullets would mature enough to produce eggs. Two hundred chickens, two hundred eggs. I believe caring for the chickens was probably my first real farm job responsibility. It makes sense, the littlest persons got to deal with the littlest livestock. So, before bothering or helping dad with the cows and pigs, I'd be headed out the door with narrowly woven wire chicken egg baskets. This would occur everyday after the school bus deposited us kids back to our farmplace. My hen house duties started around my sixth birthday.

Ground up chicken feed would be the first order of business. This would have to be carried in five gallon buckets about one hundred feet to the chicken house. Sometimes a couple of them would be needed, sometimes there might be a full one already set inside the chicken coop. The feed would be placed into long metal trays. Watering, by the time the chickens got past the little chick stage, would be easier. A large pan, probably nearly twenty inches wide and four inches deep would require a quick throw out of unused, slightly soiled liquid, a quick wipe out of residue, and then a refill straight from the chicken house water hydrant. No carrying of buckets for this part, thankfully.

On a good day, many of the chickens would, to coin a phrase, "flock" to the newly offered food and water. That left the boxes where they laid their eggs more open, easier to grab. Often a few chickens would not like to move from their nest and I'd have to get out a broom handle to help explain the situation to them. I almost often won although, occasionally, even a decent clubbing couldn't make the most stubborn hen understand.

And then, every day or two there would be one egg that had been dropped by a chicken that was roosting on the horizontal two by two boards. We couldn't just leave it lying there. Sooner or later a chicken would crack and eat the egg and that might get to be a habit, reducing production. So, being the youngest and smallest, I would often be delegated to climbing over and crawling around the roosting boards, across the feathered, pooped on, corn cobbed floor, to retrieve a two cent egg. That's just the way it had to be. It was expected.

Gathering eggs and caring for the chickens wasn't all that of an extensive or time consuming job. Birds and their poo does have an aroma that brings back memories to me to this day. However, nothing could prepare a person for the first shock wave you receive upon opening the henhouse door on a below zero day. The birds would have been in an enclosed space for eight or more hours. Perhaps the freezing air in the lungs enhanced the sense of smell, but opening that door was like a face blast of ammonia. It would quite literally take your breath away.

The smell of ammonia would make eyes water, and noses and throats clog up. Clearing the throat and spitting were common. Probably on those days my sisters and I would work a little faster, just to get out of there. It might have been on days like that, or days that I just got a little sloppy, but once in a while my egg count would come up a bit shorter than one hundred. I'd find out about that the next day when dad's morning egg gathering would exceed one hundred and twenty. Pa understood I hadn't grabbed them all, and let me understand as well.

As well as eating a lot of chicken, our farm family ate a lot of eggs. I still love eggs, not so keen about chicken. Even with a half a dozen farm humans or more consuming, we could not possibly eat in excess of one thousand eggs a week. Our neighbors would stop by and purchase them a dozen or more at a time. Twenty five cents a dozen was the going rate although one of our more affluent families always gave us a dollar for three dozen. My parents let us kids keep some of that money, I guess that's about the only way we received pay for our labors. The rest of the eggs were sold to one of the grocery stores in a nearby town.

People don't like to purchase dirty eggs. A few times a week, and definitely on Saturdays, the sisters and I would have to clean up our products. There was a metal machine that held water and around a dozen or so eggs that slowly moved back and forth, never completing an entire circle, in our basement that seemed to help. It would give the orbs a good rinse. Other residue would require a little soap, a few sponges, a little warm water, and a bit of hand scrubbing. A radio poured forth the latest songs. Still. It was boring. It was tedious. It was expected.

So, about once a week we would take large, specifically designed, cardboard boxes full of to the grocer. I'm not sure what the going rate was. Maybe it was a trade off for store bought food. Maybe some money exchanged hands. I do know that we were on good terms with the store owner and that family. We were on good enough terms that during hay-baling times, if my parents weren't able to get to town, dad would send whichever kid had a driver's license to the store and write a note to the retailer. The grocer would go to the liquor store and send us home with a six pack of beer as part of our shopping list. Illegal as all heck. We kids never drank the stuff.

A beer after a baling hay day for the adult men? It too was expected.

And that's cluck.

CHAPTER TEN
E-I-E-I-O

There were other animal noises on the farm. Woof's were common from the farm dog or dogs around. As a small child we had a collie-like pooch that seemed to be claimed by my sisters. Like all dogs I have ever known, she had chocolate brown eyes. Collie-like was called "Mopsie" due to her long light brown and white hair. She was even tempered and seemed to relish the times when she was used as a pillow by whichever children. Always outside. Animals stayed outside, always.

Okay, here were a couple of exceptions to the "outside" rule. On a few occasions baby chicks were temporarily housed in the home's basement for a week at the most until it was warm enough to move them to the henhouse. And then there was "Tammy."

Tammy was a long tailed, tan, rat terrier type that was most definitely my dog. Her short tan hair mirrored her short stature. Tammy couldn't have been more than a foot tall and a foot-and-a-half long; weighing perhaps ten to fifteen pounds. Tammy came from a litter that was born of a dog one of my cousins owned. During her first few days on the farm, she lived in a box in the basement comforted by an occasional human visitor, a hot water bottle, and a ticking clock to keep her company. She grew to be extremely friendly and patient with the exception of two things.

Tammy was an excellent rat hunter. On the night of cleaning out a pack of them from the henhouse, as chronicled elsewhere in this book, she excelled in grabbing rats by the throat and shaking them until they were dead. There was a bucket of water in the henhouse that night. After each of her successful kills, she would rinse her mouth out and go after the next rat. Pa and my brothers were impressed.

My little rat terrier had one other important duty. Sometimes after the cows were milked and released from their stanchions, they wouldn't be in quite enough of a hurry to leave the barn. That's when dad would say "sic em". Tammy would immediately leap into action and bite cow hoof heels motivating the bovine to a rapid exit. It was an amazing thing to watch. The rat terrier was outweighed at least fifty-to-one and outnumbered fifteen-to-one. Yet, she got the job done. Sometimes, after driving out the holsteins, she would have a bloody nose. Just as with the rats, a dip into a bucket of dog water would suffice.

A person might think a farm dog would freeze to death during the subzero winter Minnesota days and nights. During the extreme cold times, the canines would do what made sense. Instead of staying near the entrance of the farmhouse door, they'd make their way into the barn and curl up some hay or straw they could nest in. With fifteen cows and fifteen calves in the barn, the temperature was much warmer there.

The lifespan of an average dog is somewhere between ten to fifteen years. It's kind of a trade off for farm dogs. They had plenty of exercise, food, and fresh air. On the opposite side, they weren't coddled, surrounded by even temperatures as are some pooches that are raised indoors. Mopsie's fur was falling out in tufts as I grew towards upper elementary school age. She either disappeared or went away gradually, I really don't remember.

In Tammy's case, during the last month or so of her existence, she nested up in some barn hay and just didn't seem to move much anymore. When I was still a young teenager I came home from school one evening and didn't see her. At the supper table one of my brothers said, "I shot your dog today." Flabbergasted. I hadn't seen that one coming at all. Ma and even Pa tried to explain that Tammy was in misery and my brother had just put her out of it. I'm not sure if I yelled or just cried, but I know I left the supper table for the comfort of my room. To this day, I still hold a grudge against the lack of tact, and even vindictiveness, of my brother's words that evening. As noted in other places, a bit of being vindictive and holding grudges are part of my family's DNA make up.

My next dog came from a litter of one of our farm neighbors. They had a black and brown German shepherd male and a white samoyed husky female. The two produced at least one batch of pups that either looked like their mama or their papa. I had intended on getting one of the long haired white ones until I watched them walk through mud puddles to greet me one day. White became dirty gray quite quickly. I chose one of brown and black ones instead.

So, I became the owner of "Chad." If that's your name don't take that personally, I imagine there are dogs named "Dennis" as well. German shepherd puppies grow quite rapidly physically but not necessarily emotionally. They are still puppies, active and running all the time. It didn't help when the same neighbor we got Chad from was driving by our house one evening and dog head met the business end of the front bumper of a Pontiac. The neighbor was apologetic; he felt very bad about the incident. The result was one of Chad's ears never did stand up straight like it should. And, the dog was rather "dingy" the rest of its life.

Chad's life span was shortened in another shooting incident. The dog liked to run down to my cousin-neighbor's home and bark a lot. Dog bothered their family; they were a bit apprehensive of Chad. One night, the dog jumped its front feet up next to the house's children's window and howled. Uncle did not cotton to this maneuver. He was fed up and a good shot. One rifle round later, Chad ceased to exist. Nobody was too upset. That particular woof was not going to amount to much anyway.

About the last dog on the farm was a Saint Bernard. My oldest brother brought "Sally" out and left her there. By that time, I was around fifteen years old. I played with Sally just like any other fifteen year old would. We excelled at football where we could tackle one another. I had fun with her but had forgotten that I had a slew of nephews and nieces around ten years younger than I. When they came over, Sally was still in tackle football mode, knocking kids over. She scared the bejesus out of one of my nephews one time when Pa was close to both the house and a baseball bat. One swift swing later, Sally was one very disoriented one hundred pound woof. She never messed with the little kids after that.

There's one other incidental difference between a fifteen pound rat terrier and a one hundred pound Saint Bernard. Poo has been a common thread throughout my writing of this memoir and the topic has resurfaced once again. Tiny Tammy's dog turds were never noticeable. Sallys defecations left mounds in the grass around the farmyard. Her pile sizes might have well been the same as either the cows or the hoghouse. When mowing the lawn, there were always extra bumps to go over when Sally was around.

Sally also had an extreme fondness or perhaps penchant should be used to describe her attitude towards the pen free roosters we raised. One day I noticed her dragging and tossing about her latest victim. Looking toward the rooster's brooder house home, there were at least a dozen other's lying still. A common way to keep a dog from murdering chickens is to use wire and permantly place a dead rooster around the canine's neck. After a few days of dead poultry stench, the dog gets the message and leaves the live ones alone. I'm not sure if this method was employed here, but Sally stopped the practice after that one day's murderous event.

It bothers many people, social workers especially, to even consider the possibility of corporal punishment. Many child experts insist on "time outs" as a way to deal with a negative determinant situation. On the farm, we became experts at dog hollering. When a dog was barking during the night, one of us would open a window and yell out their name followed by a loud "Shut Up!" This rather uncouth method seemed to solve the situation. I know Sally was the recipient of some loud, nasty words just like any other dog we owned, especially by me and dad after her rooster hunt.

At some point, while I was in my late teens and working a summer job at a seed corn warehouse, my parents decided to have the farm buildings repainted. I imagine some scout had seen the dingy remnants of red still clinging to the old siding. In any event, a couple of guys showed up with a paint sprayer for a few days, the buildings looked much nicer, and the task was complete. For some reason, the main painter and Sally really enjoyed each other's company. This was about the same year that mom and dad were thinking about going to Arizona for the winter months and didn't know what to do with the dog. This made for a pretty easy solution. The last day the painter was there, he opened his pickup truck door, Sally climbed in, and dad waved goodbye to each of them. I hope they both had good lives.

As noted throughout this story, there were either bales of hay or piles of grain in nearly every building. Mice love hay and grain. Mice are adept disease carriers. Mice make good cat food. The farm had a bunch of cats that were, for the most part, a welcome addition to the number of livestock housed there. Dad would even treat them to a bowl of our precious cow milk each evening just to keep them around.

A person couldn't catch up to most of the cats that roamed the farm building site. They were too fast at running away. Occasionally us kids would tame a few down. I remember one female meow my sister named "Goofy" that would play around the front door of the house and receive all kinds of child-love attention. Goofy was gray and white. All of our cats were gray and white, with a few tabby's thrown in. I never saw a cat on the farm that didn't have hazel green eyes. The gene pool must have been limited out our way. I had found one and only one tan and white kitten in my entire years there. An enigma, I had him tamed and trained to hang around near the house with Goofy. Of course, near the house was also the car. Little brownie chose the wrong day to play under the car's engine hood. One turn of the fan belt did him in.

Cats are prolific breeders. The mama cats have two litters of around six kittens twice a year, in the spring and in the fall. Having a barn full of hay, there were ample hiding spots between bales to give birth and raise their young. My sisters and I took great pleasure following a new cat mama and watching to see into which gap in the bales they would lead us. If the cat was friendly, we'd pull out and admire the babies. That kept a ready supply of some friendly cats.

So, cats would enter this world in a barn. A half a dozen or more mama cats producing a half a dozen baby kittens twice a year. We should have been overrun with meow's, but nature, along with some assistance, kept the numbers about steady. As with the car fan belt incident, cats would bite the dust sometimes. A few of the old daddy cats, tomcats that would rival Tammy's weight and size, would actively seek out baby kitten nests and move in for the kill. Just another way of reducing the cat population.

We couldn't have caught or punished the "tom's" anyway. They were faster than a speeding bullet. Or, were they? Much to my chagrin, I eventually came to realize that either my uncle and dad, or more especially a couple of my older brothers, would initiate a "cat hunt" every fall. This is kind of sad but too many cats can lead to disease or cat starvation anyway. So, brothers would load up the shot guns and get after it. I'd like to imagine they tried to avoid shooting the few tame ones although tame ones would be more likely to be out in the farmyard. Who knows? As with dead chickens or dead piglets, they were only one quick toss into the manure spreader. More natural fertilizer for our crop land.

There was one time when my brother's shotgun skills came in very handy. Somehow a wayward skunk had waltzed its way into the farmyard. It became quickly apparent that skunk was either drunk or had rabies. It doesn't take too much brainpower to doubt the drunk rhyme. The rabid skunk was nearing the hoghouse. My sisters and I held the dogs back. My brothers took aim. That particular animal did not go into the manure spreader. We buried it and its rabies deep. It was a stinky job.

You're not reading the words of a bunch of sadistic, devil worshiping, animal killers. It just became necessary a few times. I had my own opportunities to take the life of an animal. The first time it was not my idea at all. One of our roosters had hopped up and fell into the huge cow tank full of water adjacent to the barn. I happened to see the event and reacted in the wrong way. Instead of just unhooking the fence and grabbing the poor bird, I ran into the barn and got a pitchfork in an effort to save its life by lifting it out that way. I was unsuccessful. It's tough to watch an animal die, especially when you're only ten years old and trying to save it. A few years later I had to haul out a couple of cats in the same predicament. Just somewhat the same, the cats were already dead. Manure spreader time.

I was about fourteen when the sister I was closest to age with just had to bring in a beautiful, long haired white cat that one of her friends was not allowed to keep anymore. The cat could have been owned by the queen of Sheba, she was that glamorous. White Cat was also miles away from where she had been born and raised. White Cat never did get along with the other farm felines. White Cat had a surly attitude all the time. One evening while I was in the barn, White Cat must have been ill, perhaps it had rabies, I don't know. It decided to physically attack me. After I kicked it back a couple of times, it was necessary to put an end to the attack. Of course there was a pitchfork handy, it was a barn. And, no, I did not stab White Cat. I just had to give it a good clubbing. That was the end of White Cat's life. Pa and Ma understood, they too had noticed that the cat was ill. Sister wasn't quite as forgiving.

I have to admit that I had a few cat hunts myself in my adult years. It's not a matter of being "macho," it was a matter of putting animals out of their misery. My children wanted to have cats at our place which was fine as long as they lived outdoors. Again, mama cat has six babies twice a year. We gave them away as fast as we could but would always seem to have one we couldn't bear to part with. Then, inbreeding ensues and, after a couple of years, we would have some very sick kittens. I dealt with them as swiftly and humanely as I could. We were definitely not going to go through the very, very expensive physical exams and neutering processes. They were just a bunch of cats.

If this sounds callous, remember my upbringing on the farm. They were just animals, and after my kids grew up, none of the remaining cats were too friendly. One year, while the fourth of July fireworks were going off everywhere, my .22 caliber rifle made a little noise that blended right in. The cats that survived ran away.

So what happens a few years later? I started noticing an increasing number of mice around my home. This time, we were able to get neutered and physically healthy full grown cats from an animal shelter for free. They receive my respect, are well cared for, and stick around. Only the mice have disappeared.

I was never a hunter. I don't even like guns. I found myself, at around eleven years of age, with a guitar. That's where I placed my energy into. Still, I have had to be protective of my land and family several times as an adult and have found that my .22 works better at ridding myself of unwanted creatures than bludgeoning them with a shovel—also something I had to do once.

One opossum, one racoon, two or three woodchucks, and one skunk have met their demise in my garage at my home just out on the edge of town. The skunk was the trickiest one. It required a rope, a live animal trap, and a piece of bologna to bait it. Also my .22. Luckily, I got the skunk out of the garage before it started to smell. It got buried as deeply as I could as well. Looks like I'm getting away from the real memoir task. It's back to the farm and my youth.

Sometime during my early teens, Dad decided it was time for me to expand my 4H horizons beyond roosters. Neighbor Bob had five lambs for sale. Pa had a couple of rolls of snow fencing and some extra steel fence posts. I didn't have much input into the decision. It was another of those expected jobs.

If you don't know what snow fencing is, here's a brief personal description. It is treated wood lath that stands vertically and is connected to woven wire strands. With a space of just a few inches between laths, its main job is to be placed on the west side of a farm road to keep the wind from piling drifts of snow away from the driving lanes. This stuff rolls out to be around fifty feet long, and is wired to steel posts which are driven into the ground. The steel posts are five to six feet high and need to be pounded down a foot or two to make sure they stay put. A fence post driver is used. This is a steel tube around three feet long with a welded handle on each side as well as a welded cap on the top. After pushing the steel post into position, a person slides the post driver over the top and starts banging it down. Muscle power once again.

For sheep, we fenced off the grassy portion to the northwest of the barn, out where the roosters were usually raised. A makeshift gate was installed. In went the little white lambs. Baaa! I was sent to the barn to bring back a five gallon bucket of water, then went into the granary to haul over a five gallon bucket of oats as well. Once again, the sheep were at least one hundred feet away from their food and water source. Once again, I was expected to feed and water them twice a day. Bahh! I did my duty faithfully all summer.

You might wonder why we didn't just run hoses out to the sheep or rooster brooder house. That answer is simple: hoses would be run over and wrecked by tractors, trucks, cars, lawn mowers, and other motorized vehicles. The hoses would have lost that battle. Mom and Dad encouraged me to try to work with the sheep and train them so I could show them at the county fair. 4H softball had a big influence over me, but not big enough to train a sheep.

In the end, I took a lamp I had made to the county fair instead. A red ribbon didn't mean anything to me. I was just there for the softball. And the sheep? One of them was a small, sickly animal that was not expected to live. It met its expectations. Dad and I buried it down by the lake shore. One of the healthier ones didn't survive either. I caught some heck from my Pa about over feeding the correct amount of oats and bloating that one out too far. Another lake shore shovel event.

So, I had taken care of five sheep to raise and sold only three. Buckets of water. Buckets of oats. One hundred feet away from the food and liquid dispensers. Twice a day. It was a lot of work. I don't remember how much money changed hands when the sheep were sold at the end of the summer. I do remember insisting to pay Bob for all five lambs, even the one he didn't expect to survive. Maybe we broke even.

What did this experience teach me? Well, I never had to deal with sheep again. There probably never were any extra minutes to dwell on the subject anyway. It was probably chore time again. Back to taking care of the cattle, pigs, and chickens; with a quick word or pet to goofy cats and dependable woofs.

CHAPTER ELEVEN
HAY BALES

If a farmer raised livestock, a farmer needed hay to feed them and straw to lay down for them for bedding. In the 1960's, hay balers were very expensive for one farmer to own, so oftentimes a small group of them would share the investment. In my father's case, he shared the cost with two other farmers who lived about a mile away, Bob and Dick sharing a hay baler also meant sharing hay baler labor. They each helped one another on baling days. Each of them had one or two wagons to stack the hay on so there was always another "hay rack" to fill.

Of course there was a lot more to it than that. First the alfalfa or clover hay had to be cut down from its one to two foot height. A tractor with a long extended sickle about ten to twelve feet in length made up of side to side moving wedges would be used for this. A day or two later what I would call a swather would be pulled, again by a tractor, to rake the newly cut hay into rows about three or four feet wide. Swathers employed several circular prong attachments to do this. I don't recall completely, but I think each farmer owned each of these machines individually.

The smell of newly cut hay can only be compared to the sweetness you inhale after mowing a lawn. Mowing a homeowners lawn might take a half an hour. Mowing a hayfield could take up most of the day. The sweetness of a new mowed lawn multiplied by one thousand.

On one occasion while we were cutting the alfalfa, we found a Mrs. Pheasant who had unfortunately placed a nest in the middle of the field. We didn't see the nest until after the incident. This seemed like a good time for an older brother to instruct me on egg and chick development. Whatever egg and butchered pieces from the nest leftover showed some chicks just hatched, some just about to. It didn't make any difference.

They were all dead. Mama pheasant would not be returning to this home. She flew off by herself.

That was the most serious injury that I ever saw while baling hay. Better a pheasant than a human being. Not that the inevitable scratches and scrapes didn't happen. We never took them too seriously. They were minor. The potential for catastrophe was ever present, and we were ever mindful of it.

After allowing the raked hay to dry in the sun for a couple of days it would be time to make bales. If it was rained on either a couple of more days were necessary or the bales became just that much heavier. Dry bales must have weighed at least forty pounds. The avoided wet hay could go up around eighty per bale. In other words, when I first really started helping, some bales probably outweighed me.

A hay baler was also pulled by a tractor. The baler was a rather complicated machine in that there were many different parts and functions involved. The front of the baler was made up of a group of horizontally rotating rakes that would pull the cut mounded hay from the ground. A sideways contraption would push the loose hay in about six inch wide strips into another part of the machine which would then move the product towards the back of the baler, compacting it. Once the six inch strips placed together reached a length of four feet, two strings of twine would be knotted around it by the machine. The newly formed bale would be pushed up a ramp by the next bale being produced. Thus, there was a constant supply of hay bales about two feet wide by two feet high by four feet long ready to be stacked on the wagon. The hay rack wagons were hitched up to the rear of the baler.

So, those were the jobs of the two first people in the hay baling process. My father, being older by twenty years to Bob and Dick and nearly forty-five years elder to me, always drove the tractor pulling the baler. The job of stacking the bales on the wagons almost always fell exclusively to Bob though others would help for the first load or two. Otherwise, Bob was pretty much on his own. Bob must have been over six feet tall and he was very strong. Most times he would stack the bales four layers high but if another empty wagon wasn't ready or if they were near the end of the field, there was often a fifth layer with perhaps a few loose ones thrown up on top.

I would describe Bob as a gentle giant. He was certainly much taller than I was when I was a kid. He had short, black hair, with thick arms and chest that were solid muscle. Bob's skin would tan nut brown after one day in the sun, and, as a farmer, he was in the sun a lot. During the Korean War, he had been drafted into military service. After passing his induction physical, he and the other new servicemen had been lined up and were told to count off by threes. His number was three. The induction center leader told all of the men who had the number three to step forward and follow him into another room. There they were informed that they were now in the United States Navy. I guess the ones and twos went into the army.

After boot camp, the men were sent to advanced training. The powers that be noted that Bob was very mechanically minded, Bob was trained to become a clock repairman. Timing on a ship was essential to coordinate all of the functions of a vessel. He was assigned to a ship in the western Pacific and spent the remaining portion of his two year obligation making sure every clock on the vessel had exactly the same time synchronized with all of the others. Being the 1950's, there were no digital readout clocks, no computer enhanced time equipment, so he stayed busy. After his two years were up he returned to Minnesota to start farming. Just for the fun of it, he created a clock with the numbers transposed that circled counter clockwise and told the time backwards.

So, with hay bales stacked on the wagon, it was time for tractor number two to be placed into the job. This one is where I eventually took over. The full wagons would be driven back to the farmyard to be elevated into the barn attic which was called the hay mow. A farm elevator would be used for this task. The term elevator is actually a misnomer. It brings up visions of an apartment building, business, or other high rise multi-story creation where a group of people get into a small chamber, push their floor destination buttons and are whisked up or down.

To gain a better insight into this for non-farmers would be to imagine an escalator. We step onto a moving conveyor that raises us gradually to the next level. That was more what a farm elevator was like, only without the waist high guard rails and with four inch steel blades pulled by continuous chains to raise bales or other crop items to the desired place. The farm elevator would easily reach up over twenty feet into the haymow doors. Given the angle it needed to be set at, the machine was probably forty feet in total length. The barn itself reached thirty feet tall at its peak.

As if that was not dangerous enough, a second conveyor trough full of chains and blades would be attached to the device. This part of the elevator was raised by hand power. The tractor would then be driven just past the trough and shut off. Then the trough would be lowered between the tractor and the front of the wagon full of hay.

Here comes tractor number three. It's job was to sit still and have its rear power take off (pto) gears attached by a shaft to turn the elevator chains and blades up towards the hay mow. Yes, there was usually an outside metal sleeve over the shaft that was not supposed to move to prevent things or people parts from being twisted into the machinery. It worked most of the time.

So, after engaging tractor number three's pto shaft, I would walk around the second conveyor trough, climb up on the wagon, and start placing bales onto the elevator. Besides muscle, this took some patience to time the spaces between bales so as to not overwork the person or people in the haymow.

My next door neighbor, first cousin, best friend, a year younger than me, Ken would end up in the mix here too. When we were quite young, he and I would often work the same job together. I'd sometimes lead us both into trouble, so the folks decided to separate us at times. He'd end up in the mow moving bales while I unloaded the wagons.

Ken and I devised a system of hand signals to determine if I was leaving the correct amount of time between placing bales on the elevator. Thumbs up was supposed to mean things were OK. A rapid circle meant it was time for me to speed up. A flat hand up meant slow down or stop. Usually we ended up just waving to each other so the parents put a stop to this.

Of course, the unloading of the wagon was almost always a job done in the sunshine. After the wagon was unloaded, I'd have to reverse the process by turning off number three's pto, raise the trough, and pull the empty wagon back out to the field. There was always another full wagon load ready to start the process again.

Strong and slim as a wire, Dick usually ended up in the haymow, stacking bales either by himself or with any other man or boy who could be enticed to assist in the task. This is actually where every farm kid gets their first experience at baling hay. At first, a farm kid was too young to drive a tractor so the kid would end up helping in the mow. I didn't learn how to drive a tractor until I was at least nine or ten years old, but that's another story. Needless to say, I was moving bales in the mow before then. The elevated bales would either be taken off or fall off of the elevator. People power did the rest. The bales would have to be tossed or carried and stacked in various portions of the mow. Sometimes it would take up just one section of the area. Sometimes the bales would be placed on opposite sides to help more evenly distribute their weight.

New bales were virtually never placed on top of old bales. But they were placed on top of where old bales used to be which meant walking through loose leftover hay of years or decades past. That means raising dust. Not a good place to be if a person had allergies that we, thankfully, didn't have. Years later one of my town friends chided me about carrying a handkerchief in my pocket at all times. I indicated that he had never worked on a farm or else he would have known why. There was dust or dirt everywhere to confound the nose. Nose blowing and throat clearing spits were necessary and common.

Let's face it, we were always sweaty and dirty. Even now in my later years I find it amusing to see people who immediately scrub off the slightest particle of dust that happens to appear on a hand or arm. To me, it was just a natural part of life. It was to be expected.

Or else, there was sweat to wipe off the face. It was difficult to be on a hay wagon stacking or loading an elevator with bales. These were summer time jobs that were virtually always done on warm sunny days. Believe me, it was a relief to breathe the clearer air outside, and even a bigger relief to not be working in an enclosed haymow beneath a tin roof. Whatever the temperature was outside, it could be ten to twenty degrees higher in the mow. If a body part touched the barn ceiling tin, the body part would suffer a minor burn. And we would almost always wear long sleeve shirts to keep from scratching our arms to pieces. The only good thing about working in the mow was getting a break when the ground person went to set up a new load. Yep, handkerchiefs and long sleeves worked well for wiping off sweat.

Baling hay was not always nonstop work. Every morning and afternoon a break would be taken from our toils. This was in the times before plastic bottles full of water had even been thought of. The farm family wife or children would bring out a jug of cool water to share. Sometimes we even had our own cups to drink from. Other times the workers would take turns sipping from the same water cooler nipple. On at least a few occasions we helped a different farmer who was nicknamed Festus as he resembled the character from the television show "Gunsmoke." They shared the scraggly hair and half trimmed beard look. Festus' wife would bring out a two gallon stone jar full of straight from the well water. That meant it was quite a cool temperature. There were no glasses, just a tin cup attached to an eighteen inch long handle. We took turns wiping, drinking, and throwing the last cup drops onto the field. I tried to get my drink before Festus. He chewed tobacco and didn't always offer the cleanest cup.

Noon lunch times were always a welcome splurge. Again, the farm wife or children would deliver refreshers. Workers each received their own cup for kool-aid. Bologna sandwiches and potato chips were the main course, possibly followed by a brownie. We'd sit, chat, and munch in the field for as much as half an hour before resuming our toils. Suppertimes would bring the big meal. The men would be treated to some substantial meat, bread, and potatoes along with, of course, the kool aid. This would be topped off by one six o'clock beer for the consenting adults. Just one. After all, we each had at least an hour or two of livestock chores to complete.

Baling hay took place three times each year for each farmer. In my father's group's case, that meant nine days of the summer. My dad had about six acres of alfalfa. That would get us about eight loads of hay. Each hay load had around ninety bales. Given a fifty pound per bale rate, I'll let you do the math. And don't forget that it was 1, loaded, 2, unloaded, 3 stacked in the barn. Muscles were worked. They worked even harder if the hay was damp. Moisturized hay increased the weight.

Naturally, we have to add to those totals. Our family farm also had around six acres of oats which were used in mixing feed for our livestock. Oat stalks became yellow straw which was also baled, but only once each year. These bales were much lighter both in color and in weight. After the oats were harvested in late July or early August, we would deserve this break in work effort. With chagrin we could look forward to only having one more round of baling alfalfa. Shoot, the summer looked like a breeze after that.

I don't mean to make the work of baling hay something to be dreaded. There was quite a bit of cooperation and comradery to be learned, gained, and enjoyed. This was not a time of anger or resentment. This was not a time of profiting from others. It was a necessary part of having a family farm with livestock. The work wasn't a job we were forced to do. It was a job that was expected to be done. As my father was almost a senior citizen and had the easiest job of driving the tractor that pulled the baler and hay wagon, I went along as part of a package deal. I got the next easiest job of unloading the wagons. At some point in the later 1960's Dick moved to another farm. One of my older brothers took over Dick's farmstead. Brother also took over the haymow portion of the work.

And then, the unexpected happened. I found that I could actually be paid for my labor. One of our other neighbors named Stan would sometimes ask for help. He must have been around forty five years old and would work the mow when we baled oat straw for him. Maybe dad was doing the unloading of the full wagons then, I just don't remember for sure. All I do remember for sure is that my cousin and I were placed on the bale rack to stack the straw bales onto the wagon. Neither of us were even teenagers yet. Again, thankfully, straw bales weren't as heavy as hay bales.

Stan's father must have been nearly seventy-years-old. He drove the baling tractor. At one point my cousin and I must have been near the front of the wagon finishing up the full load. Somehow I lost my balance and fell on my back off the front of the wagon. My legs were in the air and all I could see was the steel front axle of the hayrack coming towards me. There was no chance that I could get out of the way; I was going to be rolled over backwards under the metal frame which would have snapped my back bones. By some miracle Stan's elderly father was looking back at just the right time and stopped the tractor only a moment before I may have been paralyzed. I was scared. We stopped long enough for me to get back on the wagon, and the work continued without mishap for the rest of the day. Twenty five cents an hour. By the end of the day I must have made nearly two dollars.

Another pre-teen baling story happened at Dick's farm. He had an eight-year-old son to help me unload the bales onto the elevator. It was too much for the youngster to handle, heck it was more than I could handle, especially looking after the kid's well being. Dick's wife saw the potential problems, sent her son back to the house, and helped me with the unloading process. Dick had a much smaller barn with less than half a dozen wagon loads to be placed there. After two days of work he paid me four dollars.

Bob took another tack one time when baling his hay. The hay baler was used equipment when it was purchased and had a penchant for breaking down occasionally at inopportune times. There were designated "shear pins" in some spots which would break before too much pressure was applied to wreck a more important part of the machine. To guard against this down time, instead of twenty five cents an hour, Bob paid a penny a bale to his workers. His rationale was: that way he wasn't on the hook in case of a breakdown and the employees could earn more money by working faster in less time on a good day. It didn't make much difference to me. I wasn't there to make money. I was part of the package deal with my dad.

As my teenage years progressed, I found myself spending a week or two each summer with a family of cousins who farmed in northern Iowa. There were three boys in that family around my own age and, brother, could they work. They'd get telephone calls every evening from local farmers looking for baling help. And, I would go out with them the next day. We'd get the same food and drink deal as well as one whole dollar an hour for each of us. There were weeks when I'd make over thirty dollars! When I returned to Minnesota, my next door neighbor cousin and I would be called to do the same job. The Minnesota neighbors didn't take kindly when we asked for the dollar-an-hour rate. The calls stopped coming in. We didn't mind too much. We took jobs at a local seed corn company and earned over a buck and a half per hour. That was nearly three cents a minute. It beat a penny a bale.

I need to take a small step back here to explain that there was another way of getting bales into a haymow. On my Iowa cousin's farm I was introduced to life without an elevator. Their barn had a roof that extended maybe fifteen feet beyond the foundation. On that extension was a double pulley metal track set up with ropes. One of the ropes would be attached to an extra tractor. The other rope had four, two foot long steel hooks. When the tractor backed up, the hooks came down and the kid cousin's dad would jam the hooks into the ends of a group of bales. As the bales were tightly packed onto the wagon, it was possible to raise them eight or sixteen at a time.

Then, the tractor would be driven forward, raising the bales to where a point at which the steel hook contraption made contact with a metal track system that ran at a slight angle to the other end of the barn. We'd push the hooked bales as near to the stacking spot as we could, then pull a trip lever rope dumping them. One of the stackers would slide the hooks back to the barn's overhang extension as the rest of us placed the bales where they needed to be. And the process would continue. It was not as noisy as using an elevator and maybe not as efficient. The hook system was what some may call an "old fashioned" way of the time. Remember, this was happening in the late 1960's.

"Old fashioned" is a relative term. My father had loaded and unloaded hay and straw a long time before the balers I was used to working with as a youngster. I'm sure that in his early years some kind of machine was pulled through the fields by horses. I'm not sure as to how the harvesting of wheat or oats went but something was used to cut down the hay and straw. There was probably a horse drawn raking swather to mound up the cuttings at that time as well. Eventually, either steam or gas powered machines came into his life for the harvesting, but the mounds still remained.

And the mounds had to be placed into the barn's hay mow. Hayrack wagons were used to move the produce from the field into the farmyard. A transfer system with hooks, ropes, and metal tracks were used to move the hay and straw into the mow. There were no tractors during my father's youth, horses were trained to wear horse collars and harnesses, and walk forward and backward to pull the ropes.

But still, the mounds remained. So my dad, like most of the other farmers, would take his team of horses pulling a wagon with sides on it into the field. He took a long handled pitchfork as well. And, the day's work would begin. And the day's work would continue. And the day's work would end. Until the next day. Repetitive motion of raising forkful after forkful of hay or straw. The baling I was involved with as a kid could accomplish more in a day than the work he had to do in a week, and it was much less labor intensive. I could park the tractor at the end of the day. He had to care for the horses at the end of his work days.

My father had a brother about eight years younger than him. Considering that dad had taken over all of the farm duties at age seventeen, younger brother's age must have been only in the upper single digits when he became part of the hay workforce. I guess that means my uncle had an earlier version of what was to become my job several decades later: bring the empty wagons out to the field and take the full ones back to the barn. I imagine uncle got into the unloading process as well.

It was an unwritten rule for father's little brother to always bring out a jar of water for dad on every trip to the field. This was summertime work. It was hot. Perspiration needed to be replaced by fluid. My dad told me that on one occasion, my uncle forgot to bring the water. It was going to be a long walk to the homesite's well. Pa needed something to drink right now. He was the one who cared for the horses most of the time. One of the horses pulling the wagon had recently foaled a filly. Dad patted her side and said something like "Bessy, you've got to let me have some." Well trained and docile Bessy stood still while my father squirted horse milk into his mouth. My uncle remembered to bring a jug of water on his next trip to the field.

I was around that six-to-eight year-old age when one time my mother gave me a jar of ice water to take to my dad who was cultivating a corn field near our house. Being more than a bit immature, I had a fear of leaving the farm building site to walk around the hog pasture we had at the time to deliver the drink. The short cut was to climb over the fence and walk through the hog area. That too was scary. Needless to say, the hogs outweighed me about three to one and outnumbered me by about sixty to one. I put the jar in a corner and kept on playing. My mother took notice of this about a half an hour later. It quickly became one of the few times Ma was absolutely infuriated at me. I became acutely aware that I was more afraid of my mother's broomstick than I was of the hogs. I didn't have to climb over the hog fence, I leaped it. Dad got his drink. The ice had melted by then. He didn't say a word. He didn't have to.

I or we can only imagine placing loose hay or straw into a barn's hay mow. I've never seen it done and I sure don't want to start learning that job unless it becomes absolutely necessary. My father would have gotten into the mow to move the livestock greens around, that can be a given. There was one other thing I learned only through second hand information. Spontaneous combustion is a term I've heard of, maybe scoffed at. In any case, there have been instances when a certain amount of heat, combined with a certain amount of moisture, combined with a certain amount of vegetation chemicals can produce smoldering flames. Heat and vegetation in a hay mow can't be easily controlled. Moisture can be, but it's not easily done.

One thing that will remove moisture content is salt. Pouring salt onto hay doesn't damage this form of animal feed, animals need salt too. The family farm barn was over two thousand square feet. There were two interior openings, only one with a "ladder" made out of two by four lumber that went straight up a wall seven feet high. I don't know how many bags of salt went into the mow after it was filled. I do know what a bag of softener salt weighs. So, part of my father's baling experience included carrying an unknown tonnage of salt up a straight ladder and spreading it around the hay over the course of his lifetime. In the end I would have to rely on the same words I've used before—it was expected.

There are still a few barns around now at the beginning of the 21st century. Once in a while I even see people stacking hay onto a wagon. Animals still need hay and straw. Technology has turned another page. Tractors with air conditioned cabs now pull balers that will take about a five or six foot path through the field and form round bales six or eight feet tall. No, people don't lift them. The bales are still bound by twine but are dropped in the field. A tractor with a front end prong will either pick them up onto a flat wagon which is hauled to the farmsite, or grab them individually and carry them if the distance isn't too far. No roofed barns are necessary. These big round bales are just tractor stacked and then covered with rolls of plastic or tarps until they are needed. Then the same pronged tractor can move them into large round steel fencing areas for the livestock to munch at their leisure.

For that matter, many livestock operations use conveyor belts to deliver the hay to cattle that never leave their stalls. Straw? That too may become a thing of the past. If the building is warm enough, no bedding is necessary. And slatted steel floors only require high pressure washers to keep the animal waste poo away. What's the next technological advancement? I don't know. My brain is still thinking about unloading bales of hay onto an elevator. Pa didn't have to pay me. It was a job that was expected.

Dad had one rule when it came to having his children inviting friends over to spend the night. That was something like "If you're going to eat at my table, you need to work in my barn." Every couple of months I would have one or another of my town friends come over for an overnight stay. My friends would get a kick out of throwing a few hay bales around and feeding some to the cattle. I noticed that they were never around during baling days.

What happens in the evening after a sweaty baling day? Of course we'd all get cleaned up. One of my brothers had figured out a way to put a makeshift shower in one corner of the basement. That beat splashing around in a tub. Back into the living room for a little television viewing, my mother would bring in a big bowl of very salty popcorn. It was either that or glasses half full of ice onto which we would sprinkle salt and begin chewing. Salt consumption gets a bad reputation from some medical personnel. We just needed something to replace what we had sweated out during the day. Later on in my life I noticed upon occasion that, after a hard work sweat day, I would weigh as much as five pounds less in the evening than I had in the morning. That could have been true for baling days as well.

CHAPTER TWELVE
DRIVING LESSONS

Somewhere else in this document, I referred to one of my sisters who was about nine years older than me teaching me how to drive a tractor. I was around nine years old at that time. Believe it or not, that was not the first time it was necessary for me to drive a farm vehicle. It certainly wouldn't be the last time either.

Running from the farm building site down to the lakeshore was about a twelve-foot-wide dirt west to east road which we called the "lane." Lined with a bunch of steel posts and around a quarter of a mile of electrified barbed wire, the cows used to access it to wander down by the lake area where there was grass and trees to mill around and lake water to drink. That also is written about in this writing. Our lane also provided access to the lake for duck hunters and family and neighbors that wanted to go fishing. But it served another even more important function.

Farmer dad and family could drive on it to get to different fields alongside its path. The farm's alfalfa baling field was nearest the lake on the south side of the lane. Then there was a plot that was designated for raising oats, again on the south side. That left around thirty acres on the north side and sixty to the south for a rotation of corn or soybean crops.

One summer's day, for some reason, one of the older members of my family had driven the family car down the lane a ways to give an older brother a ride to the house for lunch. Brother had been probably pulling a cultivator with a tractor and didn't watch the time, almost missed our dinner session. After our noon meal, brother put me in the car and drove back down the lane to meet up with the tractor which was still in the field. I figured I was probably going to ride along on the tractor. I was wrong.

After turning the car around, brother moved its seat all the way forward and placed me behind the steering wheel. He gave me explicit instructions on how to drive the car. I was to steer it straight up the lane back to the house, just like I did my tricycle. He told me to keep one foot on the brake and to turn the engine key off when I neared the first building, a corn crib on the eastern side of the building site. Brother then started the car and put the automatic transmission in low. I complied with his wishes, for the most part.

I kept my foot on the brake. I steered straight to the building site. By that time, my parents and a couple of sisters were in the farmyard. Not being one to be shy, I decided that this was an opportunity to show off a bit. Keep in mind that I had had a great deal of practice on my tricycle. I knew how to make a left turn with it, why not the car also? So, that's what I did. Eventually I turned off the key and the machine rolled to a stop. Luckily, its forward motion ceased about three feet in front of a big oak tree that stood just in front of the chicken house on the south side of the farm yard.

I'm not sure who my parents got after more, me or brother. All's well that ends well, no damage was done to buildings or trees. The three thousand pound 1961 Chevrolet Bel Air too remained unscathed as did its six year old driver. I was directed back to training using my tricycle.

Probably the next farm implement I had to learn to drive was a lawn mower. Yes, we had a push mower and each of the kids was expected to take turns mowing different sections of the lawn. Keep in mind that our lawn exceeded the size of a football field. As the years went by, my siblings living at home became fewer and fewer until at last it was pretty much just going to be me to do the mowing. Pushing a twenty inch mower would have taken one person nearly a week just to finish it. Then, a person would have to start over just to keep up with the rapid grass growth.

Dad and Mom made an investment. They purchased an eight horsepower, thirty or thirty six inch bladed, world renowned Snapper Comet riding lawn mower. It was sweet!!! No more pushing!!! I could ride around and around the farm, making huge rectangles or circles as the land dictated. Get it all done in a day.

Of course there were glitches. One time I drove it into the swing which hung under one of our oak trees. The swing seat got caught under the mower's steering bar and I stood the Snapper up on its back end before I got it shut off. I did a similar thing when I got too close to a huge maple tree in the front yard by the road and almost climbed that one too; back wheels kept turning and up I went again.

One fun thing I found while mowing was that there was a small rise, a mini ditch, where the yard met the gravel driveway. If I ran it full speed, I could get the front end off of the ground, in other words a "wheelie". That was great fun until part of either one of the front wheels or the steel turning axle bent. Caught heck about that one. Pa and a brother managed to heat the bent part back up with a welder and straightened it out so it worked again. Brother also welded the crotch bar on my bicycle after I broke it by running the bike into a building. Twice. It was kind of a kid thing.

As the years went by I had to learn more about driving. It was expected. We had three different tractors for me to learn on and it was almost always when they were pulling something. The cattle feed bunk wagon gave way to hay racks which gave way to grain wagons. Pulling plows gave way to disc-harrows and found their way to diggers with drags attached.

When plowing, it's pretty much a straight back and forth the length of the field trip. Each time around leaves about a one foot deep indentation into the earth called a "furrow." All a person has to do for the next round is place the rear tractor tire in the furrow and try to drive straight. When discing, the driver needs to set a path that has an angle on it over the plowed field. One Saturday, Dad showed me how to do that on our land across the road; the nearly eighty acres on the west side of our farm. He was not pleased when I stopped after a couple of hours to have a snack at the house.

I went back to the tractor and did a pretty darn good job of running the machines, even finishing the forty acres next to the road. The only problem was that I didn't realize I was expected to disc the entire eighty acres. Something about being thirteen years old. Pa didn't discover my mistake until a few days after that. He had to take a weekday to finish it by himself.

It was on those same eighty acres that I learned another thing or two a couple of years later. Dad, like most of the other area farmers, had rigged up a hose system to attach to the digger. Behind the digger, a horizontal cylindrical wagon was attached. This contained either nitrogen or anhydrous ammonia, probably nitrogen. The gas was placed under the ground using the hose to nozzle system.

Pa told me to make sure that I turned off the electrically powered underground spray system before raising the digger at the end of each round or I'd both waste the fertilizing gas and get a lung full of harmful odor. I followed his instructions all but one time. Raising the digger first, it took me only a second or two to quickly shut off the electric gas valve. I'm not sure if the barf, the air being sucked out of my lungs, the instant skin shrinkage, or the eye popping dryness occurred first. That was some nasty stuff. I wouldn't recommend trying it on a dare. Like I said, it was a mistake a person quickly learns to only make once.

Pa never trusted me to do the planting or the cultivating. He must have doubted my ability to drive perfectly straight and didn't want to jeopardize cash crop production. That was all right with me. I helped out in other ways and got to goof off a little.

And yes, there were both the pickup and the grain truck to operate. As all of our land was never more than just across a gravel road which ran through it, and as we were eight miles from the nearest town, nobody said much if a teenager without a license had to drive just a bit. The folks kept me pretty close to that "at home driving" rule for the most part although by my early teens I had occasion to drive the car to my brother's farm a mile or so away to do his chores when he was on vacation. But driving tractors on the road, heck farm boys had to do that at early ages all the time.

In Minnesota and probably other states, the legal age for obtaining a driver's license for automobiles was sixteen. There was an exemption that allowed fifteen year old kids who lived in agricultural land to earn what was called a "farmer's permit" so they could drive within a reasonable distance from their home during daylight hours. Driving lessons were provided by school teachers during June and July. Being an August baby, I missed the cut and had to wait another year until I was nearly sixteen. I'm not even sure if I had a legal permit to drive with my parents in the car. That was another stipulation.

It was difficult to see most of my classmate friends scooting around our hometown when they were only a month or two older than me and I couldn't. There was always supposed to be a reason for a farm permit kid to go to town. One of my friends with a farm permit always went to the grocery store immediately upon driving to town and bought a loaf of bread so he could justifiably show any interested police officer that his was a necessary farm trip. Farm parents needed groceries too. The plan worked for him.

Yes, rules were bent upon occasion. One of these times came around my way when I was a fifteen-year-old. My youngest sister, four years my senior, had returned to the farm from college one late fall or early winter weekend. There happened to be a school home basketball game for her to take me to on one of those evenings and there just happened to be a number of members of her graduating class also in attendance. An impromptu class reunion was decided upon. The bunch that got together decided to go to another nearby town after the game for reminiscing at a pizza parlor.

Quandary. If sister took me home, she would miss the opportunity to catch up with good friends. Solution one was to find someone else to give me a ride. No other neighbors were at the game. Solution two would be to call my parents and have them pick me up. It was around ten PM. My folks would not appreciate missing bedtime just so she could get her kicks. Solution number three was obvious. She drove the car just outside of the city limits and placed fate into my own hands.

With one of my best neighbor friends acting as advisor and copilot, I just drove the car the eight miles home. I'd been driving around the gravel road neighborhood for years so it was no stretch for me to putt my way back to the farm. That quandary solved, another soon developed. By some quirk of fate, my parents were still up and about when I parked the car in the garage and entered the house. They were not pleased. Sister got chewed out even more than I did. I didn't seem to think it was that big of a deal. The folks indicated possible legal implications of an unlicensed, uninsured driver tooling around the countryside late in the dark. In any event, the 1964 Mercury found its designated parking place, once again unharmed.

That was not the only time one of my sisters got chewed out for motor vehicle operation. My next oldest sister gained permission to drive the family's 1956 Pontiac to town one evening several years before. The next morning, the first thing Pa did was to put his hand on the engine hood. It was still very warm. Big sister hadn't arrived home many hours earlier than Dad's six AM milking-time wake up. She caught heck too.

It seems in life that all things circle back around. A few decades later it was my turn to watch his offspring venture out onto the open road, or my one acre yard. The first one up was my son nicknamed "Fur". He got a double whammy but eventually turned into an excellent driver.

One evening my wife's car was parked just in front of the garage door. I showed twelve-year-old Fur how to keep his foot on the brake and just drive straight in. His braking technique worked well for the most part. He successfully parked the car without hitting either side of the doorway, but I must have had a shovel or something leaning up against the back wall. Car pushes shovel, shovel dents out the siding some. My dad has to pound the siding back in place. We never see the back wall of the garage often anyway. The dent is hardly noticeable.

It was probably most unkind of me to put the Fur into a second situation. He and I were going out to the farm to do some patching and painting. By this time, he was just over fourteen. As soon as I got off the blacktop highway near my family's farm, I switched seats with him so he could get some gravel road driving experience. It just happened to be that the car I had at the time was a manual shift, four on the floor Toyota station wagon. And we were heading up a hill. Steer, clutch, gas, shift proved to be an interesting experience. Fur got the hang of it and eventually was my go to driver so I could enjoy the ride.

Next up was my older daughter "Bug." When she was around that fourteen year old age she decided she needed to learn to drive some. Our home sat upon about one acre—the size of about two football fields next to each other. I'm no perfectionist when it comes to lawn care. Driving on the grass comes naturally to me after being raised on a farm. Bug just had to avoid the trees.

At that time, I had a used two door 1985 Toyota Four Runner. It was an early model, sat up off the ground an extra foot, and couldn't have been more than thirteen feet in length. Four cylinders didn't go too fast and an automatic transmission made for driving without much shifting. Bug enjoyed her practice time tooling around the yard and did so often. Still, somehow she managed to get the thirteen foot vehicle settled into a place where two trees about twenty feet apart, one faced her, the other was in her rearview mirror. She needed Dad to come to the rescue just that one time. Back in the driver's seat, she kept practicing and she's done just fine ever since.

Youngest daughter "Schnooks" had to have a first time just like everyone else. It just so happened that Fur and I had scaffolding set up on the backside of our house so we could do some reshingling. I had our old pickup truck parked parallel to the scaffold and we threw the shingles we were removing into the back of it. Schnooks was in the backyard when we discovered that the truck needed to be pulled ahead about ten feet to more accommodate our shingle throwing. She got elected to do the job.

Fur explained what she had to do, feet on brakes and all. Schnooks completed the maneuver but didn't quite understand how much pressure to place on the brakes. It worked out alright. The pickup truck's front bumper absorbed most of the impact as it met the tree directly in front of it. The only thing that cracked was the headlight I had just replaced. That happened about fifteen years before the writing of this document. The headlight still works.

The aforementioned pickup truck had a lot of family history to it. It's a 1974 Chevy C-10 that my dad bought in 1978. By that time he didn't drive it much. I know I got most of the use out of it. I finally bought it from my mom around 1995. With a single seat cab, an eight foot box, rusty exterior, good tires, new brakes, and a surprisingly well running V8 engine, I use it every year to haul firewood, make a trip to the dump, or get a load of gravel.

It also weighs close to four thousand pounds. Four thousand pounds of rusty steel will get the attention of other drivers. They tend to stay away from it as it outweighs most 21st century cars about two to one. And that's the first vehicle each of my children initially drove to school and back for a few months before they got their first cars. Steel protected them well.

We've all had driving lessons in our lives. It is expected. I've probably forgotten to include a few, but this will suffice. For now.

CHAPTER THIRTEEN
FUN AND GAMES

No matter what I say, living on our farm was not all work all the time (although it seemed like it quite often). There were always days, especially during the summers, when either friends or family got together and enjoyed themselves.

As I grew up, there was an area of interconnecting gravel roads which we called the "block." It was not the size of a city block. Our block was about six miles around. There were eight or ten farm houses with driveways hooked up to the block. It just happened to be that eight boys about my age lived in some of those houses. One family had four boys. The eight of us, and a couple more that lived just a bit further down the road and around a corner or two, would chase around on our bicycles as frequently as allowed by our parents.

The "block" roads were pretty much all on flat land with only an occasional small grade to push the pedals a bit harder on. It was the 1960's. Kids were safe enough on their bikes. Car and truck traffic occasionally had to be worked around but there were no near collisions. Let's face it, the population of our nation doubled over the next sixty years. Twice as many people, more than twice as many cars to dodge now. Back then, the neighborhood moms and dads took turns keeping track of us.

Sometimes our group of boys would push their pedal limits. We'd bike over an extra half mile to the north where there was a most serious hill with a narrow gravel road to contend with. The farm land near the hill was so steep that it was only good for pastureland. It would have been nearly impossible to plant a crop on it. The planted seeds would have been washed down to the bottom. Animals in this pasture needed water. That was no problem as an artesian well always flowed near the bottom of it.

This natural well had some of the cleanest and freshest water. It constantly flowed. Still does, but I wouldn't drink from it any more after fifty years of farm chemicals being sprayed around.

So, the gravel road next to this hill was also a steep grade. Being kids, we'd create great thrills by biking down it. One of the guys had a speedometer attached to his bicycle. On one trip down, the instrument indicated fifty-miles-an-hour. Getting to the bottom of the hill was of course a huge thrill. As we were at that indefatigable preteen age, we'd push the bikes back up a couple of times or more just for the rush on the way down.

I imagine that we all slept well after days like this.

Somewhere else in this work I've included a portion of our "block" that had a creek running through it. (As any real Minnesotan knows, the word "creek" is actually pronounced "crick.") Some of the acreage around the "crick" were naturally running downhill and weren't much good for farming other than as a pasture for cattle. There were just too many trees to knock over at the time. So, given a stream and a small forest, there was a great deal of room for kids to hop over a fence and rost about. Everyone had a cap pistol or toy rifle. It was a perfect training place for us to play "army" and rat-a-tat-tat after one another. As far as I remember, I was the only one that ever actually landed in the "crick." Got my feet soaked. Glad the other kids were there to pull me out.

Quite often us block kids would end up at one neighbor farm or another. During the winter, somebody would cajole a parent into driving us over to the four boy family place. They had a barn haymow with little to no hay and we'd often spend an hour or two dribbling, passing, and shooting basketballs at a hoop attached to one of the interior walls. Even during below freezing weather, we'd work up a sweat.

Summertime baseball-softball games were often a biweekly get together. One of the area farmers allowed us to play in the yard of an abandoned farmsite he either owned or rented. Usually though, the kids ended up at my farm yard. There were always two or three kids batting and when they made an out, all of the field players would move up a position, the pitcher would move into the batting role, and whoever made the out was relegated to the outfield. Quite often, after a game of work-up, mom would have a pitcher of kool aid and a plate of cookies available. In any event, there was always a water hydrant and a hose to quake the thirst.

Camp outs were another way to entertain either farm or town friend visitors overnight. Sometimes a tent was even used. Usually though, we'd end up in the part of our farmyard between the house and the gravel road. Mom had strung a stiff wire between two evergreen trees there for a clothes line. Pa always had a canvas tarp around for covering a wagon full of grain. If it was not employed for this purpose, it became fair game for tweens to throw over the clothes line. Tie a few bale twine strings to pounded-in wooden stakes. Instant tent. Well, just good enough to keep the dew off its inhabitants for the night.

It's nice to sleep outside with friends when you're that age. Chat until you're too tired to talk anymore, then snooze. The only concern, beyond shooing away the occasional cat or pooch, was for the safety of the happy campers. It was the 1960's. There was no threat. If we had to move into the house, who had the house key? There was no lock on the door anyway. Locks didn't appear until the early 1970's when my parents began spending winters in Arizona.

Another good camping spot was down by the lakeshore. Sometimes we'd take a few minutes to pitch a real tent. Sometimes kids just drove down and slept in their cars. If it was just a couple of kids, we'd again employ dad's tarp and his pick up truck with the side gates up. Throw the tarp over the top, once again instant tent. It was relaxing, listening to the nightcall birds and the steady lapping of the lake water.

Growing up on a farm, I could name the type of many birds by their calling sounds. After years of city life with thousands of cars traveling by, I can only recognize a few.

During my late teens and early twenties, the lakeshore also was a favorite destination. Sometimes I'd take a sweetheart there to listen to the car radio while we played kissy face, huggy bear. Other evenings it would be party central. There was always plenty of wood around for a campfire. There was always a twenty-one-year-old around to buy a keg of beer. Nobody had to drive home those nights, so it was a fairly safe situation.

Decades later, I'd take my own kids on that lake-pickup-truck-with-a-topper excursion. My kids had grown up near a town. The experience just wasn't the same. Maybe that had something to do with a change in toileting routine expectations. Stepping behind a tree came naturally to me. Not so for my kids.

And, there was always a boat pulled up on the lake shore area. The first one was a flat bottomed conglomeration that we would paddle out past the lake shore reeds to go fishing. Sometimes it was a few family members. Other times it would be just a friend or two. We'd catch bullheads, about the only fish the lake contained at that time. That was the fun part of fishing. I never cared for the beheading and cleaning of the bullheads. Even a marvelous cook like my mother couldn't beer batter her way into my taste buds enjoying the muddy lake water flavor of what little meat we'd get from them. And, the bullheads had tiny little bones that were virtually impossible to avoid. On fish meal nights, I'd find the peanut butter jar.

One of those flat bottomed wooden boat days, a town friend came out to the farm to spend a couple nights. He and I somehow rigged up four broomsticks as posts on the boat and covered it with an old blanket to reduce the inevitable sunburn threat. The first day was great. We had a transistor radio tuned into a rock and roll station and managed to fish and waste an entire day on the calm water. The second day was more interesting.

With high hopes of a repeat experience, we set out from the shore on a morning of gentle breezes. By the afternoon, the wind came up and knocked over our blanket covering. With larger waves lapping, I tried to oar our way back to the shore. The friend I was with was a bit of a rascal. He pushed his oar the other direction. Soon we found ourselves in the middle of the lake and eventually ended up on the opposite bank. Ma was not pleased when we had to telephone her for a ride back. A couple of days later, she had to drive Pa and an uncle over again to row the boat back. The two men didn't mind their time on the lake. Ma had an uncharacteristic scowl on her face for a few days.

The Dobie fishing beach area was quite a local attraction. It was almost always open for friends, family, and neighbors. Most of the time, people would just drive into our yard and take the dirt road lane down to the lake for an afternoon of enjoyment. Sometimes they'd stop by for permission. More often they'd stop at the house on their way out for a quick chat or to drop off excess fish they'd caught or one or two too many ducks over their legal limit they had shot. It was a matter of sharing the wealth.

Again, the lane was just a hard dirt path. If Dad deemed it too damp to drive on, he'd keep people from attempting the trip through the mud by placing two old white sawhorses across the path. People got the message.

My fishing stories pale in comparison to the one in which my uncle and father told. At some point, they were clearing away some old stump trees down by the lake, using dynamite. I guess it was easy to get that explosive years before my time on this earth. As the end of their working day came, they realized they were getting hungry. One lighted stick of dynamite got thrown into the lake water. An explosion later, they collected all of the bullheads they could carry. They ate well that night.

Somehow during my early teens, a better boat was available. Though it was still made of wood, it had curved walls and actually moved nicely through the water. An attached gas engine took some stress away from rowing. There was actually a small island down near the north side of the lake. One evening, a half a dozen of us boys decided that an island camping excursion would be appropriate.

By the time we had the boat loaded, it was starting to get dark. I gave the duty of running the boat motor over to one of my friends and stood at the front of the boat with a flashlight. There were the remnants of two trees that had grown in the nearly dry lakebed during the dust bowl 1930's that we had to go around. We successfully spotted them and made a landing on the island. A quick tent set up, a quick wood fire, five kids, and an old iron pan pre-filled with popcorn, oil, salt, and butter made for a lasting memory.

I'm not sure if it was the next day or the next year, but once again the same group of teenage boys found themselves out in the same boat on the same lake. This time I had taken enough foresight to bring along an old wooden toboggan, the kind you use for snow sledding in the winter. With a rope hooked to the back of the boat we attempted to use it as a water ski. It was great fun, for about twenty feet. Then the boat motor fins would get caught up in lake weed and required shutting down and cleaning off. We gave it a good try anyway.

And life jackets? I don't believe anyone owned one at the time. Even given a lake as shallow as we were on, it's still a wonder no one was ever found floundering about.

Again, decades later, I found leftover construction material; a piece of plywood and a bunch of one by twelve inch lumber. Screwed, painted, and caulked together, my son and I introduced my wife and daughters to our version of a flat bottomed boat. Same lake, different results. My wife and daughters are just not lake water people.

So, the lake was another place or thing to do. Our side of it was a mucky, muddy, weed infested affair. On the northeast side, where the island was, there were actually some areas of sandy beaches. Much more desirable. Still, I'd swim off of our shoreline through the underwater weeds, and pluck off the occasional bloodsucker I'd find attached to a leg. The best way I found to swim was, believe it or not, underwater. I'd dive into whatever waves I found and push the water weeds out of my way as I pulled myself into the deeper water.

I had a couple of nephews about seven and eight years younger than me who had grown up just a couple of blocks away from their town's municipal swimming pool. They could outswim anybody, all day long. Then they came to stay with my folks for a few days when I was about nineteen or so. A swimming trip to the lake was called for. Those kids knew about pools, but not about swimming under the water. When I was challenged to a race, I dove under. Pretty soon, I had a couple of eleven year olds hanging onto my shoulders as I walked to the more shallow shore line area. I'm not sure if they ever went swimming in the lake again.

But that was the early 1970's. Swimming in a lake couldn't really do anyone any harm. Maybe they're too polluted by chemicals from farms and towns now to be safe for swimming.

As a young child, there were a few family ball games and picnics down by the wooded area next to the lake. Pile a half dozen kids into the back of the pickup with a water cooler and a woven basket full of sandwiches and off you go. (By the way, there is NOTHING better or more fun than riding in the back end of a pickup truck.) Of course, the wooded area I'm talking about here was at the end of the farm lane. You know, where the cows went to graze grass during the day time. It wasn't difficult figuring out where the bases were for our family softball games. Just pick out four cow poo piles and try not to slide into them.

Okay, maybe we'd get confused at times. There were lots of cow poo piles.

I was very young at the time of these "drive to the woods" family events. By the time I was five years old, my brothers were all out of the house and on their own. A few years later my two oldest sisters were gone as well. I guess the attraction of a glass of kool aid and a bologna sandwich just couldn't hold their attention anymore. We've all had our moving on times.

Another family get together tradition of that time was "Visitin." About once a month or so, one or another of my parent's brothers or sisters would show up at our farm place on a Sunday afternoon. Quite often no company was expected that day. No one was ever turned away. The men would sit in the living room and slowly chat. The women would brew up coffee in the kitchen and talk up a storm. Being a young child in those situations, I'd soon lose interest in an uncle talk. I also didn't drink coffee. I suppose I'd find my way to my upstairs bedroom and play with toys until chore time.

Maybe I just resent the vistin' times because I couldn't watch TV when the men took over the living room.

I feel a little bit bad about being the annoyance I was to my parents. There would be prearranged times when they would visit with friends or relatives on a Saturday evening. By that time, my brothers were out of the picture and my sisters were either on dates or resented my brattiness. I had to go along with the folks. Once we arrived at our destination, the host and hostess would scrounge around and find a few of their grown children's leftover toys for me to push around and make imaginations with. One of my uncles had an old guitar that a son in law had left at his house. That kept me enthralled for hours. To this (writing) day, I still have about a dozen guitars at my home now. Some toys really hit the soul. But that's another book

At some point, probably before my time, a person with the last name of Dobie and a person with the last name of White were married. So, I grew up with the annual Dobie-White summer Sunday family reunion being held. One year, we would meet in a park in northern Iowa. The next year, we would meet at a park in southern Minnesota. Considering the location of our family farm and the attraction of a large farmyard and a lake for kid type people to flaunt around in, there were many reunions I didn't have to drive to. As there were several distant cousin boys about my age in attendance, we always had a good time.

A good family reunion. I have the feeling they're more difficult to come by these days..

The last Dobie-White family reunion I remember attending was in 1986, of course on our family farm. I doubt they still occur.

And a Dobie family reunion? As far as my siblings go,that will never happen. And they can point the finger straight at me if they like. I don't even care which finger they use. Some things just should not happen, but they do. That might find its way into another chapter. I guess it should be expected.

CHAPTER FOURTEEN
HORSEPOWER

"Dad, can I get a horse?"

"No, God bleep it! I'll never have another crow bait hay burner on my farm."

I guess that kind of ended that discussion. At least for a time. I'd ask the same question the next year and receive the same answer. Pa had walked behind, cared for, and cleaned up after enough horses while farming as a young man to last him the rest of his life. I'd be disappointed year after year, but I can't blame him for his bleep response. We had enough mouths to feed and enough poo to scoop the way it was when I was growing up.

You'll have to excuse dad's "bleep" words. I think both his temper and cussing was a direct result of inheriting Grandma's vindictiveness. But, that's just my personal opinion.

During the 1950's, it was a whole lot easier to start up one of his orange Allis Chalmers tractors instead of a horse. Didn't have to harness them first. And, they usually started right up with battery power, though they each had a bolt apparatus on the front of them if hand cranking the engine over was necessary. It was never necessary.

That wasn't the case with Dad's first machines. Early 20th century cars needed a hand crank to start them. And during the winter in southern Minnesota, that could present a problem. Below freezing temperatures produced cold engines that resisted turning over. Pa had to explain to me how he, and most others, would place a dozen or so corn cobs under the oil pan of the car. Next would come a half a cup of kerosene or coal oil. After a bit of time for soaking in, a match would light the mixture and it would give off a smoldering heat. A half hour later, the oil pan and engine would be warm enough to hand crank over. It was not a spur of the moment that would send one to town on a whim. The process took about an hour before they even got out of the driveway. If they weren't snowed in.

Needless to say, the cars and trucks of that time did not have all wheel drive. Only one of the back wheels would produce the power momentum either forward or backward. Dad never did have a four wheel drive vehicle. I didn't get one until the late 1990's when I was 45 years old. How did we ever manage without it?

Speaking of being snowed in, Dad would keep our barnyard driving spaces open by using a tractor with a scoop bucket on the front. The bucket was only about six feet wide and he had literally hundreds of feet of driveway to clear. We'd watch him all bundled up with his teeth gritted together facing into the freezing wind while he drove. Ma was concerned for his health. County and township snow removal trucks didn't make trips into farmyards. We were on our own.

Dad's Allis Chalmers WD 45 was about a 40 horsepower, 4 cylinder tractor. It had a wide front end, with the two front wheels set about four or five feet apart. His WD Allis had somewhere between 20 to 30 horsepower. It also had 4 cylinders, but it had a narrow front end, front wheels just a couple of feet apart. They each had steel seats with a spring underneath them to prevent some of the inevitable jolts made by a bouncing tractor driving over rough terrain. Pa had a thick padded seat cushion he just moved from tractor to tractor, depending on which one he was driving at the time. I never understood the rationale about the advantages of the front wheel differences. I'll leave that to the implement dealers. Either way, they both pulled machines in and around the farm. It must have made a difference as to what horsepower was needed to pull what implement.

To put this into perspective, 21st century cars often use a 2.0 liter (122 cubic inch) four cylinder engine. The 2.0 can generate around 200 horsepower. More perspective: when I was twenty years old I purchased a car with a 5.6 liter, 340 cubic inch engine which produced 250 horsepower. Step on the gas pedal, pop the clutch, squeal the back tires. Just the thing for a somewhat rowdy young man. Would it top off at 135 miles per hour on a straight, flat, five mile stretch of rarely used tar road? That would be illegal.

My first recollections of the orange machines driving across the fields vary from season to season. Dad probably pulled a four row planter during planting season. It would take a lot of trips down and back to plant seed in a field nearly a quarter mile long and nearly a quarter mile wide. This was usually a late April to mid May job. By June, the planter would be put away and Pa would pull a four row cultivator to clean early weeds between the new corn or bean rows. He had rigged up an umbrella to keep the sun off of him on these trips. More trips. Many trips.

Summertime would see the Allis Chalmers work continue. There was hay to bale. There was a bunk wagon to pull feed out to the cattle. There were occasional trips to town pulling a wagon full of corn or beans to sell if the commodity prices were good, or if money was needed no matter what the going rate for grain was.

In the fall of the year, the Allis would pull a two row corn picker with a wagon attached to it to harvest the corn. Many more trips up and down the field. The other Allis would run an elevator and drop the corn, cob and all into one of our three wired steel corn cribs. The wind would blow through them to dry out the corn. Enclosed steel bins required natural gas burners to push dry air through them. Another expense. This eventually became a necessary evil.

Enclosed steel bins don't just appear. They have to be put together. Just another example of groups of farmers working together. Pre-drilled steel would be delivered. Huge, thick concrete circles twenty or more feet in diameter would be poured. A half-dozen men and kids with punches, wrenches, and leather gloves would arrive to follow accurate plans. In a matter of a few days, another bin would be erected. Teamwork.

Scratched arms and fingers, just like baling hay or any other farm job. Suck the blood off of the oops and spit it on the ground. Won't feel it again until the end-of-the-day shower. Yeah, we were in one sense thin-skinned people. We bled easily. But, we were thick-skinned enough not to notice scrapes and bruises. Even then bandaids were rarely used. Scratches just scab over. A few days later the scabs fall off. It was no big deal. It was just another thing that could be expected.

By the way, empty steel bins make great echo chambers for teenage boys who want to play guitar and sing songs in. Again, that's another book.

On the other end of the spectrum would be full grain bins. Shelled corn that had been lifted into the bin by an elevator or an auger would slide off to the sides for the most part but there was always a big pile in the middle. In order to completely fill the bin, a person had to climb into it with a shovel and push the center pile towards the outside edges. A dangerous job. A person should have a rope tied around their waist or armpits to keep from being sucked down under the corn kernels. I was lucky although I had to dig myself out of over-the-knee-deep-danger several times. To this day, this shoveling process costs the life of a farmer on a yearly basis in southern Minnesota. Safety harnesses are sometimes unwisely overlooked.

As long as we're on the corn topic, later in the year another machine, also tractor powered, would be used to separate the corn from the cob for either selling or to be ground into chicken or hog feed. We'd end up with quite a pile of corn cobs in the process. We'd also end up with callouses from either shoveling or forking the cobs. Corn cobs made good bedding for the chicken house. I imagine some of the cobs found their way back onto a field if necessary. More natural fertilizer.

In the early 1970's I attended college and had one required class of Environmental Science with about forty other students. At that time, the word "natural" was a big buzzword; everybody wanted natural ingredients whenever possible. When the instructor asked the class what natural fertilizer was actually made up of, only a few of us raised our hands. I guess most non-farm kids didn't realize how much animal poo was spread to fertilize their deliciously edible natural foods.

I can understand that that might have been quite a shock to the majority of the class members. I didn't bother asking any of my city friends what happened to their poo—we all flush. In small town Minnesota cities, dried out human residue ends up as field fertilizer too. It's only natural.

Before I poo us all out about poo it should be noted that in southeast Asian countries it was only polite for a guest to leave a little of this natural fertilizer when one was invited over for a meal at someone else's house. They too used natural human fertilizer, as well as whatever duck or other animal dung they could get, to work into their small rice paddy farms. A few acres could feed a family year round. Being natural crosses country boundaries.

Pa always kept one old-fashioned wind-dry grain bin. We needed it. He didn't separate the corn from the cobs for cattle feed. The cows needed the extra roughage so they would eat feed that ground up cob and all.

Following the harvest, a chopper would be pulled through the fields. Think of this as about a four or five foot wide lawn mower deck. Either it would have a few blades under it, or a "flail" system of small sharp iron strips attached to chains that could knock down whatever went underneath it. The corn picking machine never took down the entire stalk, leaving about two feet of stubble to be knocked over before planting, hence the chopper was necessary.

Fields that had been chopped would next be plowed. Given the smaller amount of horsepower the Allis Chalmers tractors had, they were probably lucky if they could pull a two or three bottom plow across the fields. That would amount to at most a three-to-four-foot-wide strip each way. More rounds to make.

Usually, the weather would hold well enough that the ground would be ready for the next breaking up of the ground process. This time a disc harrow with multiple vertical circular steel wheels followed the tractors. The next step was using a digger, a toothed attachment with a finer tooth drag pulled behind it. The digger work usually ended up being spring work. We were more than satisfied if the land was plowed in the fall before the snow fell.

Sometime around 1960, the WD 45 was traded in on a newer International Harvester 450. Still with four cylinders, the dark red IH would wind up to around fifty horsepower. It seems to me that it had a wide front end on it also, though I can't be sure as my next door uncle had a similar IH. Maybe his had the wider wheel base. Anyway, the 450 had a traction lock which could be engaged by pushing a foot down on a steel pedal by the tractor's brake pedals. I'm not sure, but I equate that with being like a positraction rear end drive on a pickup truck. Both back wheels turned with power at the same rate and time. This red tractor also had something called a "Torque Amplifier" which somehow enhanced its power. Again, I'm not sure what it really did but, as a kid, it was fun to sit on it in the yard and yell "torque amplifier" and shove a lever forward as cousin Ken and I played our games on a non running machine.

There were quite a number of different tractor manufacturers during the first half of the 20th century, some of them consolidated names and colors and survived into the 21st century. Some of them are now only collectors items with a challenge to find parts for. There were various colors of orange, shades of red, and at least two hues of green available. One of the green lines made the biggest impression.

In the early 1960's, John Deere corporation introduced a new line of tractor creations. Gone were their days of making two cylinder "Johnny Pops" which sounded horrible but produced enough power for many farm uses. What I would call the 10 series was manufactured. 1010, 2010, 3010, 4010. Different sizes and horsepowers for different needs.

Wouldn't you know, one of my older brothers had been a mechanic for an implement dealership that worked with John Deere. Brother's hands became irritated with the cleaning solutions used in tractor repair. Brother was moved to the parts department. A few years later, the implement manager retired. The other parts department person didn't want the job. Brother became the manager. There's more to the story here. Brother can tell you about it.

Being a good son, brother brought one of the 3010 (pronounced thirty ten) models to pa's farm for a weekend. Being a good salesman, brother brought one of the 3010 models to Pa's farm for a weekend. Everybody won. Dad purchased the fifty horsepower, four cylinder machine. It officially belonged to Dad. It unofficially became MY tractor. It was a beautiful color of green. The 3010 had eight gears forward and at least two reverse, all controlled by a right hand side shifter that was placed near the fender. Yes, I could still run the Allis WD and could find my way around the IH 450, but the 3010 was what I was going to drive.

And drive it I did. Like the other tractors, it could go at a twenty mile per hour clip in high gear with the engine running full throttle. It was what Dad would send me on to help out a neighbor when needed. The 3010 was also what I used to pull a plow around the field. And there were many autumn times when I'd get off of the school bus around four in the afternoon and I'd find the John Deere already attached to the plow, waiting for me. Usually willingly but sometimes needing the prodding a teenager requires, I'd be in the field, following Dad and his red IH 450 from one end of the field, a quick turn around, and back to the other end of the field. Almost always until it was dark. There were a few nights when it would be nearly ten PM before we'd quit.

The John Deere would pull a plow with three, sixteen inch blades. The IH 450 pulled four, fourteen-inchers. Between the two of us, we could turn over almost twenty feet everytime around the field. It would be November in southern Minnesota. There might be a snowstorm coming in. The work had to be done. It was expected.

One thing those tractors didn't have were cabs over the operator area. They were mostly open air machines. Yes, Pa did put what he called "heat housers" on them. These were steel rod supported canvas coverings over the engine that flared out around the front of the driver's seat. There was even a plexiglass windshield applied to take some of the sting out of the cold air. The heat housers worked remarkably well when a person would be driving into the wind. Some of the engine heat would find its way back to the operator area. When driving away from the wind, there was no heat. There was only the stinging of dirt flying up against my back.

All things considered, the JD3010 wasn't completely my tractor. Pa would claim it during the early summer cultivating time. He'd rig up an umbrella again and would work all day. I think he even attached a radio to one fender.

The 450 International Harvester, all fifty horsepower of it, was the mainstay of the family farm for most of the 1960's. Brother still ran the John Deere dealership. By the end of the 1960's the IH was replaced by a JD 4020. Its ninety horsepower nearly doubled the IH 450. And, the 4020 had a six cylinder diesel fueled engine. Pa had to purchase a different farm fuel tank as everything else ran on regular gas.

There were a couple of other perks to dad's 4020. It had both an AM radio and a cab over the driver's compartment. No, the cab covering was not insulated, heated, or air conditioned, but it did keep out most of the rain and some of the dirt. The drawback was that it didn't keep out much of the engine noise. Perhaps it even amplified it. No wonder I have hearing aids as an adult.

Time to sidetrack again. As our farm bordered a lake and was pretty much open to anyone looking to fish or hunt, an interesting event was about to unfold. One late fall day I was plowing the north thirty acre spot, I believe with the 3010, when a good sized flock of geese settled in on the freshly turned over ground. A couple of geese hunters saw them land.

Now, the geese didn't pay no never mind to the tractor and I, they were just happily minding their own business and I was minding mine. That's when I saw the two hunters in the farmyard. I have no idea who they were, but they determined the best way to get to the geese was to get down on their bellies and army crawl their cradled shotguns out to the field. I'm not sure if they noticed me and the tractor or not. Hunters can be very intent on their purposes.

I've never had any interest in hunting. I didn't like the "wild" taste that came with that type of food. If I had to, I'd shoot a pig or a cow in the head and just get to it. Pork and beef still work better for me. I've never really had any interest in guns either though I've had to protect my building site from an animal or six at times. This goose hunt was an entirely new conundrum for me.

As said before, hunters were usually welcome to go down to the lake. However, on this one day, the hunters were pointing shotguns at the geese in particular and at me and my tractor in general. They were getting close to the geese. I was near the line of fire. Decision made, I stopped the tractor and ran the throttle back and forth until I heard a most satisfying backfire boom. Geese flew away. Hunters, I don't know whether they shook their fists at me or just cussed. I couldn't hear them anyway, the running tractor noise was too loud.

With more horsepower from the 3010 and the 4020, bigger implements could be pulled through the fields. I seem to remember an eight row planter and an eight row cultivator being acquired. These would have been about twenty-four feet wide. Nothing wider than that would have fit into the quonset style machine shed anyway. I suppose wider disc harrows and digger - drags followed as well. The 4020 should have been able to pull a five-bottom, sixteen inch blades each plow. That's almost fourteen feet each round. A big improvement.

Dad kept the Allis WD around for farmyard use even after the advent of the green John Deere take over. The orange Allis was smaller and a little bit easier to maneuver when taking the feed bunk wagon to the cattle. It was always the tractor we hooked up to the elevator for lifting hay bales into the upper story of the barn. And, eventually, it would power a grain auger to pull grain from the ground up into the storage bins. One of my brothers ended up with a WD. it could have been the same one for all I know.

"Dad, can I go out for the football team?"

"No".

Football was played in the late summer and early fall. More trips to town to pick up the kid after practice and games. A chance of the kid getting hurt. I heard them all. Left unsaid was that I needed to be around the farm to help with the harvest and field work.

Combine horsepower

It wasn't all tractors that had horsepower on the farm. I've already written about the pickup truck and grain truck that had a straight line six cylinder, 235 cubic inch, gas powered engine. They produced between one hundred and one hundred fifty horsepower each. The two trucks got a lot of use.

And then there was the combine. A John Deere of course, it was introduced to the farm somewhere around 1960 as well. There might have been two of them at different times as the need arose, I don't remember for sure, but it would make sense.

The reader of this document can look up pictures and specifications of a John Deere combine. I'll just try to give a person a snapshot of them. They were big machines with four foot high front tires and at least six welded rod steps up to get to the driver's seat. A large grain hopper was placed behind the driver's area. There was an auger attached to it to transfer the grain to whatever wagon or truck that awaited at the end of the field. The wagon or truck would make the trip to the farmyard, that was another person's job. When harvesting, Pa kept the combine moving through the field. The rest of us, most often me by myself, just had to keep up transferring wagon fulls to the huge farm grain storage bins.

The term combine probably came from its multi purpose use. On our farm, it could be used to harvest oats and soybeans when the "bean head" was attached to the front of it. This would be about a twenty-foot-wide mechanism with a back-and-forth serrated edge bar that would cut the grain stalks just a few inches from the ground. The grain would be pulled into the combine by use of an entry auger and from them all sorts of belts, gears, and pulleys would separate the grain from the stalks and leaves.

Machinery magic.

Once the August oats and September soybeans had been harvested, the bean head would be unbolted and the "corn head" would be attached. The first corn head we used would pick and shell four rows at a time. This was a big improvement over dragging a two row tractor powered picker through the field. Eventually, Pa acquired a six row corn head. Fewer trips back and forth across the field. I don't believe dDad ever got one that would pick eight rows at a time. One that size probably wouldn't have fit into the machine shed.

My father was always quite possessive of the combine. He probably didn't think I could drive straight enough to properly pick every single stalk of our crops. Any advantage was needed for maximum yield.

So, I'd be the one driving the 3010 pulling wagons from the field to dump them into the grain bins. I'd have to lift the bottom part of the grain elevator up out of the way, drive the tractor and wagon past it, then lower the elevator bottom back into position as the wagons most always were emptied from the back. Hydraulic hoses, steel reinforced heavy duty rubber hoses with steel ends, would be hooked up from the wagon to the tractor. High pressure hydraulic fluid would be forced from the tractor to the wagon's hydraulic arm and the front of the wagon would lift, dumping the grain into the elevator.

It worked pretty well except that the wagons were usually about six feet wide and their rear grain opening doors were less than half of that. Scoop shovels were employed getting all of the grain out of the wagon's back corners. That's what the kid was for. It was expected.

And, let's not forget that the John Deere 3010 would be running for its hydraulic pressure. Meanwhile, the Allis Chalmers WD would also be running, turning the elevator or auger. Two horsepower machines at one time. One operator. It kept me or whoever else was hauling the grain pretty busy. The danger of machines, chains, and rotating power take off shafts kept me or whoever else was hauling the grain on our toes.

At first, getting those one hundred bushel or so wagons into place for dumping into the grain hopper without spilling might take a little extra backing up or moving left or right a bit. After the half-a-dozen trips, it was easier to spot where the tractor and wagon wheels left their grooves in the grass and the job got easier. (A bushel is about the same size as eight gallons for the uninitiated.)

I have to interject some information about backing up farm implements here. Pretty much everyone has seen a semi truck driver backing a trailer to a loading dock or around a corner. That takes a certain amount of skill and practice, especially when considering the driver is doing this deed by using only a couple of rear view mirrors. I can't do it.

If you haven't done or seen that, you've probably noticed or participated in backing up a camper into a parking space, or maybe a boat down to the water edge. In each of these situations a person has to turn the steering wheel left to make the trailer turn right or vice versa. In each of these situations the trailer is supported by a single fixed wheel axle. These axles don't steer.

There are a bunch of types of farm machinery that have single, fixed wheel axles that don't turn such as balers, plows, cultivators, and disc harrows to name a few. That's not true with grain or bale wagons. Those have front axles that turn depending on which way the tractor is going. Backing them up, a farmer has to look to the rear and double steer, right becomes left which becomes right again. The steel "tongue" of a wagon extends around five feet to where it is attached by removable bolt hitches to the tractor so there is some margin for error. All too often, the tractor operator has to pull forward to straighten out the trailer and tongue, then try again. An advantage a farm tractor operator of the 1960's era had was that the tractor seat was somewhere between three to five feet off of the ground. Good for viewing.

It gets easier after a few thousand times.

Wouldn't you know, just when I thought I was getting good at reversing a wagon into just the right spot, one of my brothers had to upstage me. He was driving a tractor, pulling a single axle hay baler, with a double axle baling wagon attached to the back. Somehow he perfectly backed up all five axles to the waiting elevator so we could finish unloading the last of a hay crop. Show off.

The harvesting process I've briefly described here was the reaping end result of a year's crop production. I've touched on several other parts of the farm operation in other places. Baling and walking beans help could be provided by neighbor kids if needed. But, fall harvesting of the crops was one of the two times of the year when every farm kid between the ages of six to sixty was called home to help. The other time was during crop planting time.

Planting would usually take place during the month of May. Sometimes a few farmers would get a head start on the job, but never before April 15th. That's the first date that crop insurance could be in force. In southern Minnesota, April plantings were rare, it all had to do with the temperature of the ground, air, and weather forecasts. There is a story about a farmer checking the earth temperature to see if it was warm enough to support seeds. Farmer would drop his shorts, and sit on the ground. Warm enough for the butt, warm enough to plant. Dad never did this, as far as I could tell, but he would pick up a handful of dirt from time to time in the spring, just to feel it.

Mom and dad were "old school" farmers. They would often check the calendar for moon phases before planting. Ma always insisted on planting potatoes after the third quarter of the moon so that the seed taters would grow down instead of "going to tops," unwanted leaves. She seemed convinced that too much shining of the moon would reduce the size of the legume crop. Pa would also note the moon phase. He wanted the extra shine for above ground crops—corn and soybeans.

Are you skeptical as to the effectiveness of "planting by the moon"?
Maybe.

Are you skeptical as to the moon's effect on ocean tide movement? Moon and ocean cycles have been scientifically acknowledged. Are you skeptical as to the moon cycle or weather pressure systems' effect on people? Ask any school teacher. They can attest to the amount of a young person's energy level being more enhanced when the moon is nearly full or if a low pressure system is advancing into the area. If both of those things occur at the same time, students can get to be quite a handful.

There's a lot more to decision making than farmer's instincts. They'd have to consider how many growing days a variety of corn would have, 100 day growing days, 110. 120? In any event, the corn was always planted first. I suppose the soybeans had an eighty day growing season to maturity. Ground already smoothed over by the tractor pulling a digger with a drag attached to it, the kids would be called in.

And the boys showed up to help. The pickup truck would be filled with bags of seed corn. Dad would center his tractor on the west field approach driveway, with the centerline marking of the tractor hood pointed directly at the tallest tree he yearly aimed at on the west end of the property. Bags were dumped into the planting hopper holders which fed a steady stream of seeds into each row and off Pa would drive. He always did the planting. Didn't think I'd drive straight enough for this either. It's a different story in the 21st century. Not much line of sight planting goes on. High-tech tractors sync up with Global Positioning Satellites and straight rows are assured without much human steering involved.

In the 1960's, planting would go on all day, for as many days as it took. The sons always helped.

Then, along came May of 1972, when dad's still eighteen-year-old college freshman son drove the 25 miles home after classes to help. That was a spring of a great deal of unrest concerning the war in Viet Nam. Unwinnable, with a fortune of both money and young men paying the cost. Afghanistan and Iraq were still three decades away. As a country, we hadn't learned a lesson about limited warfare or insisting on installing democracy in a feudal system nation. Despite the best efforts of patriotic young people—and their lives. More trillions.

Yes, I was a member of a group of thousands of draft age young people who joined in peaceful, anti-war demonstrations. People can choose their own political stands. But on Friday, I was there to help plant corn. One of my brothers also came to assist. He had been out of the Air Force for about ten years. Short-hair-trimmed brother told me how he and some of his American Legion friends were talking about going to the college and teaching some of them "effing" hippies a lesson or two. My locks of hair touching my shoulders, I told him us college kids had a name for him and his friends too: "effing" rednecks.

Viet Nam was in a civil war between the north and south parts of their country. Much like the United States Civil War. Brother against brother. This became apparent that day.

Sometimes people just have something to say. He stayed on his side of the corn planter, dumping seeds into the hoppers, I stayed on my side doing the same. There was no need for words for the rest of the day, week, month.

As long as I'm this far off topic, I'll relate a couple more situations regarding the attitudes of young people—high school students. As a teacher, when discussing war with kids in the late 1980's, many students would sardonically say "Just nuke 'em." Then along came Iraq's invasion of

Kuwait and the need for United States military intervention. These same "macho" kids became very nervous and started saying things like "I don't want to have to fight."

Flash forward about thirty years. President Trump was sputtering about the country of Iran. There was talk about reinstating the draft. This time the possibility of drafting young women was even discussed. I was still teaching school and noticed yet another change in student attitudes. Whereas before the event, the youngsters were talking about prom dates and social drama, their discussions turned to nervous chatter and serious concern about being thrust into battle.

No, I was not in the only generation that was concerned about mandatory induction into military service.

I could have written another chapter about planting. It would have been a short one. I have digressed from a fun writing of tractors and such. Filled in a few paragraphs with opinionated politics. Back to the horsepower as this chapter was intended.

John Deere kept up with the 40 line for about a decade. Sure, we had a 4020 but the manufacturer morphed into creating the 4030 and eventually 4040. Somewhere along the line, the numbers changed and I don't know what to. I'm just writing about my experiences in the 1950's, 60's, and 70's. After all, this is just a memoir. Not a lot of research on my part.

The horsepower machines I drove all had inflatable rubber tires. The big machines in the early 21st century look more like army tanks. Like tanks, many employ wide continuous tracks that sit on each side of the machines. Military tank tracks are made of metal. Farm tank style tractor tracks are made of wide, steel reinforced, very hard and strong rubber. Steering is done by virtue of hydraulics. I have no idea of the horsepower their engines produce but I imagine it's considerable. And the size and width of the implements they pull are incredible by my 1960's era standards.

Six row corn or bean heads? Things of the past. 21st century corporate farms use semi trucks with forty foot long flat trailers to haul the planters and harvest heads. At least forty feet in width. Less trips across the fields. Very few wagons left anymore either. Semi trucks again. Pulling forty foot box trailers. Sitting at the end of the fields.

Still, I just can't help but remember the derision I received from my older brothers about how much harder they worked than I did. Well, there were three of them, all teenagers when I was born. Maybe they did work harder. In my time, I was usually the only one running the machinery and the shovel. Maybe they just didn't have access to as much horsepower.

CHAPTER FIFTEEN
SILAGE

Silage is basically chopped up corn. Stalk and all. This was an early to mid-September job, when the corn stalks were just starting to turn a mixture of green and brown and the corn cob kernels were near the crunchy phase. A farmer would use a tractor to pull a machine across the field that did the actual chopping. A person with a second tractor pulling a wagon followed along the side. There was an auger on the cutting machine that would push the chopped up corn into the wagon. This required some close coordination between the two tractor operators.

As I was usually back in school in September, I didn't get in on much of this picking. The schoolbus wouldn't drop me off until close to four PM. By that time, most of the silage chopping work was done. But, there were Saturdays when I'd be in on the task.

It took more teamwork than just the two in the field. When one wagon was full, another person on a tractor with a second wagon would be ready to fill up a load. A wagon full would be hauled to the farmyard, backed up to the hopper of a flail machine, also powered by a tractor and an extra man. This second flail machine would be an expensive one to own. I'm sure Pa was a part owner with at least two other farmers who also raised cattle. Either that, or Dad rented a day's labor of the man and machine. In any event, labor was often traded between farmers.

The machine that threw the silage into the silo was quite an operation. I can't tell you just how it worked, but it was amazing to watch. It had a curved chute at the top and would literally throw tons, and I mean tons, of damp, green, heavy cut corn stalk pieces above the edge of our silo where clumps of the silage would land with precision into the silo's fifteen foot opening. By the way, our silo was about average height of those in the area. It stood about thirty feet. The machine had quite a throwing power challenge. God forbid that anyone or anything got in its way.

Also like most other farms in the area, our silo was constructed of curved, vertical concrete wedges. These had strong steel rings bolted around them about every three or four feet running horizontally. The cutting and flailing and filling of the silo was usually accomplished in one day. I'm not sure how many acres of corn were used. The silage produced would be used to feed the cattle for an entire year.

There were exceptions to this rule. Maybe it was extra hungry cows. Maybe they were overfed at times. Maybe we couldn't make the silage on time due to the weather. Whatever the reason, there were a few times when we'd run out of silage.

There might be a week or more when Dad and I would drive the pickup truck out to the corn field. Armed with machetes, we'd cut off enough green stalks as close to the ground as possible, throw them into the back of the pickup until it was full, then unload the produced supply onto the feed bunk wagon. This was usually a procedure done after the milking had been completed. By that time it was evening, going on dark. I imagine Pa would save half of the pickup load for the morning feeding, although he may have had to machete his own load the next day while I was attending school.

As I've written somewhere else in this work, the silo was attached to the barn by a silage room. This was just a walled and roofed in concrete floored addition to the barn where silage could be thrown down to. The silo itself was an open roof structure. A closed roof could have allowed noxious if not deadly fumes to be trapped inside. Silage was picked somewhat green and had a high moisture level. I don't know about spontaneous combustion. Its likelihood would have been advanced with a closed ceiling.

Running up the inside of the silage room to the top of the silo was about a thirty inch curved tin steel chute to make sure the thrown silage hit the correct part of the floor. Next to the chute, there were a series of about thirty inch by thirty inch wooden panel doors that could be removed one at a time just to give the guy in the silo access to the metal chute. Slowly, over the course of the year, we'd remove one panel after another until we just plain ran out of silage.

It was a lot of forking silage. And, Pa did probably ninety percent of it.

Dad used about a two foot wide fork, with teeth around four inches apart to move the green goo. The fork handle was only about three feet long. Most often he'd end up in the silo by himself although I did my fair share, believe me. I imagine he'd keep track of the number of forkfulls he'd toss down so he'd know when there was enough for the feed bunk wagon and barn use. Sometimes he'd forget the number and would holler down something like "Do we have enough yet?"

It didn't take me too long to figure out that I had to either have a good eye for the required amount or at least tell him we needed a few more forkfuls. Pa didn't like it when I underestimated and either he or I would have to climb back up the perfectly vertical steel ladder that hugged the silo wall. Sometimes I either didn't answer quickly enough or dad would decide to toss an extra scoop or two. It happened at times that I'd stick my head into the chute to yell an answer up to him about the same time as a forkful was headed down.

Sure, I'd get a face full of silage once in a while. It was expected. It was better than getting in the way of a face full of poo. When cleaning out farm buildings, that happened too. Poo happens. Unexpectedly expected.

Sometime around the mid 1960's Pa purchased an electric silage unloader that worked most of the time. This was mostly a horizontal machine. A horizontal frame was attached to two horizontal wheels which pushed up against the interior circular silo walls. They slowly made their way around the inside of the silo. Again, horizontally placed augers would pull the silage to the center of the machine. Finally, an electric motor would shoot the silage out of a curved, vertically placed assembly which was always aimed at the chute, and down would fly the corn mixture.

The electric silage unloader was operated using a couple of switches located in the barn attached silage room. Maybe it was just one switch to turn the thing on. I'm just not sure if there was a cable system to raise and lower the machine when needed, or if gravity pushed it down into the corn mash.

Most of the time it saved a lot of trips, climbing up and down the vertical steel ladder. Most of the time it saved a lot of forking silage down the chute. However, our farm was located in southern Minnesota. You know, where temperatures could dip to nearly thirty degrees below zero some days. An open roofed silo filled with a damp corn mixture was a prime target for frost and occasionally snow.

Frozen silage meant a trip up the ladder anyway. If the electric machine just buzzed, or shook, or blew out a fuse, that was a big heads up. Time to send the kid up with a five tine fork to break up the frostiness. Dig down a foot, holler down to Pa, try the machine again. It might take two or three attempts to be successful. There were a few times when we'd just give up and start forking, the old-fashioned way.

As noted elsewhere in this document, getting the silage out of the silo was just one step in the process. Whatever came down had to be hand forked either onto the feed bunk wagon or to a large cart we pushed inside the barn for distribution between munching cows while they were being milked or thrown out into the calf (and sometimes bull) mangers. Still, when the electric silage unloader worked, it saved about half of the forking.

There were and are much more high tech auger systems for moving silage, grain, and ground food available. They use a great deal of electric energy. If a part breaks, systems fail until repairs are done. That's why the huge animal factories of the 21st century employ maintenance men. I never saw a twelve-inch-long steel fork tine break. Replaced a few of the wooden handles, though.

We didn't have any memberships to a fitness center. Hard, calloused hands came from working with wood handled shovels and forks. We didn't develop the bulging, manly muscles a person might see at a fitness center. Still, there was something about lifting twenty-pound forkfuls of silage at least one hundred times twice a day. Blood veins would be pushed to the top of the arm skin during the workdays, then reduce during the night time. Our arm muscles turned into long, strong sinews. The same as our leg muscles. Walk around the farm yard. Walk around the fields. Climb twenty feet straight up on a vertical steel ladder to get to the silage.

No time for a fitness center. Didn't need one.

One of my brothers complained years later that the boys in our family all seemed to have bad backs that ached from time to time. He credited it to all of the lifting and physical labor we did on the farm when we were young. Sometimes people just have to have something to say. I figured it was all just expected.

CHAPTER SIXTEEN
THE HOUSE

I'd wake up in the morning and could tell which way the wind was blowing without even opening my eyes. North wind brought a cow smell. East wind brought a hog smell. South wind meant chickens. Yes, I had the south bedroom on the second story of our farm home.

The house was built in the T shape that most homes were designed in during the late 19th and early 20th centuries. Think of looking at it from above. The top of the T faced the north. The second level of the home was actually technically only a half a story. The outside walls were four feet tall and followed the roofline up to about eight feet in the center. There was enough space for two beds and a few kids in each upper bedroom.

On the main level of the house, the top T was around thirty feet wide and twelve feet in length. The northwest room was the living room. That's where the TV was—I hung out there a lot. I probably hung out there a little too often after a room sized air conditioner was placed in the north window. It made for a cool place to watch the TV. The temperature in the upstairs of the house was determined by open windows, a couple of fans, and wind movement. Ninety degree days would be followed by eighty degree nights.

The north east room was Ma and Pa's bedroom. It was to be avoided by the children. Folks need their privacy. Sliding down south of these rooms, in the narrower part of the T, next came the dining room. It was probably fifteen-by-fifteen and held a sewing machine, a bureau for the fancy plates and napkins, as well as a huge maple table that could reasonably seat a dozen people when the extra extension leafs were added to the middle. It's good that it was that large. Ten people lived in the house at one time.

On the southwest corner was a bathroom I've described somewhere in this memoir—about six feet by six feet. Between the bathroom and the dining room there was a rather narrow, thirty-inch stairway leading to the second story. There was also a hallway at one time which allowed easy access between the stairway, bathroom, and kitchen.

The most important room was located on the southeast side. That, of course, would be the kitchen. Originally it would have been about ten foot wide and ten foot deep but a house expansion turned an old porch into an extended fifteen in width. That's where the food was. I hung out there a lot too. There was even a "smaller" kitchen table set up on the east side of the room. It would only comfortably fit around six or eight people, depending on how many little ones were around at any one time. And, believe me, there were a lot of little ones. I became an uncle at age seven and my brothers and sisters produced over a dozen, any of which would find their way in for lunch at one point or another.

On the upper level there were four bedrooms. The northwest room of the T was the place where the "girls" (sisters) slept. Grandma claimed the northeast room. A smaller guest or big brother room was nestled against the western wall in the middle of the upstairs. There was a hallway on the east side connecting all of the rooms to the stairway. And then there was the south room. It was the premier bedroom in the house as it had windows on each of the south, west, and east sides. That was where my big brothers were placed but again, they were teenagers when I was born and had pretty much vacated the space for me to grow up in.

At one time, the basement had been a place to fear, dirt walls, brick floor, and all. Naughty children were sometimes sent there to consider their sins when necessary. I don't remember that part of it as, by the time I could remember, we had a full, concrete block basement with a concrete floor. The long main room on the west side was big enough for a huge chest freezer, an old kitchen sink, a wall with hooks full of work coats, caps, and coveralls, a couple of old tables and chairs, and in the middle of the room; the crown jewel; the pool table. I hung out there a lot too.

Side note here. What did the work coats, caps, and overalls have in common? For one, they were always plentiful. Not much got thrown away. We also worked outside in all conditions and learned to layer up. Secondly, most of the outerwear was dirty. At that time, these clothes were bulky. Between their bulk and tendency to collect grease spots, they would wreak havoc on a clothes washing machine. They weren't cleaned often. What the heck, the next day they'd be dirty again. Of course, those dirty clothes were not to be tolerated in the main part of the home. Ma made sure both kids and non-work clothes were clean.

And the third thing the clothing had in common might go unnoticed by some people. Just about every item had the name and logo of a seed corn company sewn into it somewhere. It was a good trade off. The seed companies got free advertising and the farmers got free outerwear. Sometimes a new seed corn cap would be placed aside for more formal occasions like going into town, but most of them earned farm sweat and dirt, wear out, and would be replaced in a year or three.

There was an old joke something like "Why don't farmers wear tennis shoes? Because seed corn companies don't give tennis shoes away." There was some truth to that until the mid 1990's when Northrup King seed company actually came out with footwear bearing their logo.

As long as we've gone this far on a sidetrack, I'll add in a little more footwear knowledge. I grew up wearing lace and hook style work boot shoes that ran over the top of my ankles. Pa wore the same, heck most farmers all did. I learned a trick from dad about getting good forming boots. On the first day of getting a new pair, we'd walk down into the lake and get them good and soaked up. After a day wearing them while they dried off, the footwear would most definitely be formed perfectly for our feet. I don't know if that is a recommended technique, but my feet never have given me much trouble.

Back to the basement.

The southeast corner of the basement held the water softener and water heater as well as an improvised shower stall and a bunch of shelving for our farm produced canned vegetables. An east room had no windows but a desk and more shelving provided space for Mom's Stanley Home Products business.

On the northeast side, there was more old furniture, shelving, and a little clutter. But, it was the northwest room that held the important stuff. This was where the firewood was stored. Approximately twelve-by-twelve, it would be restocked to the ceiling every fall with enough carbon producers to keep the house warm all winter. I was still young enough that I wasn't much help on firewood stacking days. It was another situation where my brothers would later tell me how much harder they worked than I did. I suppose they got in on a lot more cutting and splitting of firewood than I ever did. I'm not so sure about the splitting as, to the best of my recollection, the wood furnace door would allow about a sixteen inch wide log two feet long to be thrown into it. Usually more than one piece went in at a time. Every few hours, Pa would throw in more wood, even during the nighttime if it was needed. On cold nights, it was often needed.

A huge wood burning furnace separated the northeast and northwest rooms. Just above it was a three foot by three foot iron grate. The living room, the dining room, and the downstairs bedroom would warm up nicely. With rather an open floor design, most of the downstairs would be reasonably well heated. That couldn't be said about the second level

Cold winter winds in Minnesota most always come from the northwest. Why would the "girls" room be on the northwest side of the house? Both it and grandma's northeast bedroom had grates in the floor to allow heat that flowed straight up into them from the basement furnace. My room at the south end was not so fortunate. There was about an eight inch circle cut into the floor, covered with a smaller grate. That was my heat source. The south room was just above the kitchen. During the winter, I'd wake up to the smell of coffee. And a little heat.

Oh the ironies of life. Somewhere around 1963, Ma had had enough of the wood furnace. The folks decided to join the 20th century and had a natural gas furnace installed. It had a strong fan and ductwork attached to better reach all of the rooms and the downstairs was quite comfortable. The upstairs bedrooms were still a bit cool. The sisters' and grandma's rooms had heat ducts placed in them. The only way to run ductwork into my south bedroom would have been through the bathroom. I declined. It was better to just keep my eight-inch grate in the floor. I smelled coffee in the morning. Bathroom smells might not have been quite so invigorating.

The gas furnace did a fine job, as long as the electricity was on. A huge snowstorm a few years later knocked out power for several days. That was a time that would try kids' souls. My next door uncle and his family didn't have power either. And, they had a newborn baby girl to keep extra warm. Somehow, probably through the use of a tractor and bucket, uncle and Pa got to uncle's house and their family moved in with us for a few nights. We'd bundle up and sleep two to a bed just to keep from freezing.

And baby girl? By a stroke of fortune, when they took out the wood furnace they neglected to take out a small wood fired parlor stove from the basement that was still attached to the main chimney. We could still get warm food, and baby slept in a well blanketed cardboard box not far from the only remaining heat source. We survived. Baby thrived. Made for a good story.

The biggest downside of the three day power outage was doing the required outside farm chores. Uncle and Pa had to milk all fifteen cows by hand. As youngsters they had plenty of practice. It took an extra hour twice a day, but the task was completed.

All through the years, the house stood and was well maintained. Walls were either repainted or hung with new wall paper. The floors, which had all been linoleum when I was a child, gained carpeting in the living room. When it was time to recarpet, the old ones were removed, recut, and placed into upstairs bedrooms. And so it went on. And so the family went on for many years of occupancy.

And occupy it the family did. As noted before, there usually wasn't a lock on the house doors. Even if they were locked, the kids all knew where the spare key hiding spot was in the barn. We could get it, and we would be welcomed in. There was always food in the cupboard and a spare bed or two upstairs.

Whichever kid was in college at the time would leach off of the folks for free room and board during the summers; although each of us worked summer jobs too. Youngest son hung out there during summers until he was twenty one But, there was always a steady parade of others who spent time there too.

It might just be one of mom and dad's children and their kids would spend a few days vistin' the folks. Maybe someone would have to get away from an arguing spouse for a while. Maybe someone would have a high pressure situation and needed to return to the farm to pause and refresh for a few months or so.

A couple of times, my parents would welcome one of their children and their entire families to stay for extended periods of time. These would be times when one of my brothers or sisters had either sold or left one house and had to have a place to stay until the next home was vacant for them to move into. All were welcomed. All were fed. All were housed. There was never any bill.

One early April day, nineteen-year-old college sophomore son didn't feel well. He went to a doctor, was diagnosed with mononucleosis, and received a shot of penicillin. Didn't realize I was allergic to penicillin. During my teenage years, I had often wished that I could just have all of my pimples at one time and just get over it instead of a couple here and a couple there. Sometimes even bad wishes come true.

Hive rows of pimple rash began at the bottom of the feet up to the neck. Laid out on a farm bed, tears free flowing from my eyes due to the pain and itch. Mom rubbing calamine lotion deeply, repeatedly, selflessly while I shook from freezing fevers. Her tears flowed freely too. I don't remember much of April and May of 1973 except that Dad moved the couch out of the living room and put my single bed there. I barely remember the baking soda baths, sleeping endlessly; and any time that I did wake up, mom would deliver as much scrambled egg sandwiches and chocolate milkshakes that I could devour. I could only consume those mild foods. Parents were worried, the kid was still not eating enough and losing weight. It went on for weeks. Thank the parents for seeing through a successful recovery.

A large irony. One month I'd be having college friends partying in the farm house. A couple months later, my folks were saving my life.

Dad passed away around the first of November in 1989. Mom continued to live on her own in the farmhouse, with a great deal of help from me and two of my brothers that still lived close by. The rest of my siblings had all hightailed it to the Twin Cities and were over one hundred miles away. By the fall of 1995, Mom's medical situation required her to move into an assisted living facility in a town about ten or twelve miles away. The house sat empty for a few years. I had been the member of the family that was expected to move out to the farm. By a fluke of chance, that happened.

In the summer of 1999, I was basically ordered to apply for a teaching position in my old home town by one of my former farm neighbors who needed help with the bunch of kids she was mentoring there. At first, I resisted even applying for the opening, but a person doesn't argue when the lady, who was like a big sister to me, says go. Interviewed, I received the teaching assignment. This was the fourth school district that I was going to be teaching at in four years. Had I known it would last the rest of my working life, the end result might have been different.

I moved my family to the farm in August of 1999. Most of the farm furniture was still in place. We added some fresh interior paint and installed some new carpeting in the bedrooms. It was to be our new home. Sort of.

We still had our previous house to deal with. There was little interest from buyers for it. Renting it out turned into quite a fiasco as well. My son was a senior at a different school and wasn't interested in changing for just one year. He drove twenty five miles a day each way, five days a week. And my beautiful wife, Babe, also had to drive twenty five miles to get to her job which really was the mainstay of our family employment situation. She'd be out the driveway by 6:30 every morning and wouldn't get home until around 6:00 in the evening. I was still taking one college night class each week, an additional twenty five mile trip one way, and playing with a band on weekends. Somehow we managed to drive seven hundred miles a week.

Any winter in Minnesota is a tough one for transportation. That wasn't the worst weather winter, but it was trying enough. Son put his car in a ditch at one point. Luckily, it was close enough to my brother's house to get a tractor tow out. And at the end of the work day we would end up in what was an old country house, with no insulation and substandard wiring. We couldn't plug in electric space heaters, circuits would blow. The furnace was over thirty years old, it just couldn't keep up either.

Now, let's throw in some outside forces. Siblings. Especially siblings in law. People who hadn't grown up there, had no ingrained love for the land, and had put forth no sweat equity into it. They knew that money would be changing hands at some point. As one in-law put it to me; "Then we'll split the money evenly, after paying for whatever renovations you put into it first." Eye dollar signs can be very influential. There'd always been a family member or six waiting to take a bite out of me. Now, I'd just say they can all bite me.

We left the farm on April 1, 2000. One of my nieces moved in immediately for the summer. There were a few people that rented the house over the next several years. Eventually, a nephew moved in. I feel horrible for my part of the family dynamics that ended it all. It honestly is all my fault, and that's something I'll have to bear the rest of my life.

During the state fair of 2008, a couple of my brothers and a couple of my sisters accepted an award for being owners of a "century and one half" Minnesota farm. Six months later, it ceased to be.

I guess five generations of a family having lived in one house should be quite an accomplishment. There should have been more. I tried to keep it but was met with a few lawsuit threats from family members. After it was sold at an auction, I tried to buy it back. It wasn't to be. The house and other buildings sat empty for a few years. Now, all that's left is a few trees.

But they won't be there for long. Inevitable? No, unexpected and unnecessary. I know how Judas felt. In the end, I took my thirty pieces of silver just like all the rest. Haven't spoken to the siblings since. Bitter? Very.

Just in case you are wondering, my siblings' kids are welcome to anything I have or any help I can give them at any time. My no contact situation applies only to their parents.

CHAPTER SEVENTEEN
OVER-ROMANTICIZING

That's the term one of my children told me when I'd reminisce about growing up on the farm. I guess I can understand the kid's point of view. My children didn't get to grow up there. They'd just get in on all of the painting, patching, and repairing I did to the farm buildings. I did a lot of that and had them help me also. Must not have been too romantic in their eyes. They couldn't possibly remember what I did.

The size of the farm yard alone was equal to about three football fields. This was lit by a single, one hundred watt light bulb up on an electric pole in the center of the building site. The bulb was rarely on.

It was so dark outside on the farm that on a non moonlit night a person couldn't possibly consider counting all of the stars in the sky. On a cold winter's evening, after chores were done and we walked from the barn to the house, dad would point to the north and show me the lights from the aurora borealis. I'm still so bothered by town streetlights that I have to put blinders over my eyes just to get to sleep.

It was so quiet on the farm that the rare car that happened to drive by would be noticed. But, we didn't pay any attention to them as they passed us. There was a curve in the road by our house so automobiles had to slow down, it wasn't a trail to vroom on. Usually, the silence would only be interrupted by an infrequent animal sound. Maybe the noise of a pig using its snout to open a tin feed tray and then again as it dropped closed. One could even get used to sleeping through the roosters morning crows.

I ended up buying a place near a highway. I became somewhat used to the steady drone of traffic. Siren laden vehicles wail by several times a day. Difficult to get used to that. A fan next to the bed to drown out the worst of it during sleep times.

Our farm was a park. Lined on all sides by groves of windbreak trees. Never more than fifty feet from a rope swing, an improvised ball park. Next to a sandbox. Perfect for kids to play on once they scooped away the cat poo that had accumulated overnight. On the other side of the tree, a fifteen inch deep kiddie pool. Perfect for hot summer days. Perfect for dunking the youngest brother's face under the water. Scary fun.

Our barn was a gymnasium. Ladders to climb. Bales to turn into secret hideaway forts and tunnels. There were huge wooden support beams to balance on. Ropes leftover from olden baling days still hung from the metal tracks that were attached to the rafters. Perfect for Tarzan swingin,' complete with the ape screams.

Our farm was a vacation destination. A five minute bike ride to the lake. Camping, fishing, boating. One of my brothers had taken an old, inoperative elevator, covered in lumber and plywood. A perfect dock for shooting off illegal evening 4th of July fireworks over the lake. A week's worth of summer warehouse work pay gone up in trails of sparkling fire and booms. Worth every penny. Take the boat out the next morning and pick up the spent floating rockets.

December ice fishing shacks. January one car with a rope attached pulling toboggans and sleds filled with kids across the ice. Quite a thrill, especially if you're sitting on the saucer, the last sled in the line. Wide turns, Incredible speed.

Our farm was the best restaurant that could ever be imagined. Cold milk over morning cereal. Or, bacon and eggs. Who needs cooking oil? Fry them up using lard, another animal ingredient we could render on the farm. Keep the bacon grease in the frying pan. Use it as cooking oil for lunchtime's fried potatoes. What's for supper? Beef, pork, chicken. Maybe the meat came from my favorite calf. Snowball was an all white moo, an oddball in the herd of black and white holsteins. Sister used to make sure I held that thought in my head from time to time. Fresh vegetables as well. A smorgasbord of excellence in country cooking. No one ever walked away hungry. They may have walked away to do more work, but never hungry.

Our farm was a zoo. A half a dozen different species of fur and fowl. Hundreds of mouths to feed. They fed us too. Some were pets running around free. Most of the penned animals just moved off to the side when someone walked through their domain. I can hear them. I can still tell what kind of animal's around just by their scent. And the smell of their poo. The aroma of money on the hoof.

Our farm was a racetrack. Slow pace races in abundance. A slow pace plowing fields in the chilly autumn. Same speed can be said for planting, cultivating, and harvesting. Ride the lawn mower around and around the yard. Good practice for when you'll be big enough to drive the tractors.

Then it's a fast race on the bike to visit the neighbor kids. Come on over to my place, we'll race around the circle drive at our farmyard.

Our farm was an orchestrated crop rotated exercise field. The fields seemed endless. Millions of plants giving off their oxygen in the early morning. Walk through them. Just walk through them. Peace in the world. Hoe in hand.

Our farm was a meeting place. Friends, neighbors, family; most all were welcome at any time. Nephews and nieces crawling all over me. They'd race their bicycles, trying to beat my car out of the driveway.

Our farm was a business. A perfect blend of family, crops, animals, and machinery. Make sure you have more than one plant crop, make sure you have more than one type of animal to sell at some time of the year. You'll never know for sure which commodity will have a good price, or little profit. Don't count your chickens before they hatch. Don't put all of your eggs in one basket. More than just colloquialisms. Common sense.

Our farm was a 20th century farm. A couple of hundred acres and livestock to tend to. Things were evenly balanced. The 21st century brought thousands of acres under one or another family's control. All corn, sometimes. All soybeans, sometimes. Or maybe build huge animal operations. All hogs, sometimes chickens, could be, maybe it's cattle. Huge animal factory operations, thousands of heads of animals, with little land. Animals that never left their stalls to roam around outside. Or, huge field farms, thousands of acres, with little livestock. Manure for fertilizer became a cash crop. Especially when grain prices needed for feeding the livestock were high, it might be the only money maker. The stench doesn't bother a person. Especially when they don't live on that land. Let the neighbors complain, we're a corporation. We live in town, or a building site miles away. A different world.

But, most of all: Our farm was a way of life. We lived it to the fullest extent possible. We really lived it.

It's difficult not to over romanticize just a bit.

Just one guy's opinion of heaven on earth. I hope there's black dirt in heaven. I pray for it every night. Every night.

PS God, I'd also pray for a guitar there. But, that's another book.

Now, what's left to write about except some sophomoric poetry about life's experiences. But, that too is another book.

Over Romanticizing. It was expected.

ABOUT THE AUTHOR

Dennis grew up on a farm in southern Minnesota. He is a retired school teacher and musician. Dennis substitute teaches when he is not traveling south with his wife. He helps build or renovate houses for Habitat for Humanity both in Minnesota and South Carolina. Dennis is the proud father of three adult children.

9 798844 208836